# Regex Quick Syntax Reference

## Understanding and Using Regular Expressions

Zsolt Nagy

Apress®

*Regex Quick Syntax Reference: Understanding and Using Regular Expressions*

Zsolt Nagy
Berlin, Germany

ISBN-13 (pbk): 978-1-4842-3875-2        ISBN-13 (electronic): 978-1-4842-3876-9
https://doi.org/10.1007/978-1-4842-3876-9

Library of Congress Control Number: 2018953563

Managing Director, Apress Media LLC: Welmoed Spahr
Acquisitions Editor: Steve Anglin
Development Editor: Matthew Moodie
Coordinating Editor: Mark Powers

Cover designed by eStudioCalamar

Cover image designed by Freepik (www.freepik.com)

Distributed to the book trade worldwide by Springer Science+Business Media New York, 233 Spring Street, 6th Floor, New York, NY 10013. Phone 1-800-SPRINGER, fax (201) 348-4505, e-mail orders-ny@springer-sbm.com, or visit www.springeronline.com. Apress Media, LLC is a California LLC and the sole member (owner) is Springer Science + Business Media Finance Inc (SSBM Finance Inc). SSBM Finance Inc is a **Delaware** corporation.

For information on translations, please e-mail editorial@apress.com; for reprint, paperback, or audio rights, please email bookpermissions@springernature.com.

Apress titles may be purchased in bulk for academic, corporate, or promotional use. eBook versions and licenses are also available for most titles. For more information, reference our Print and eBook Bulk Sales web page at www.apress.com/bulk-sales.

Any source code or other supplementary material referenced by the author in this book is available to readers on GitHub via the book's product page, located at www.apress.com/9781484238752. For more detailed information, please visit www.apress.com/source-code.

Printed on acid-free paper

# Table of Contents

About the Author ............................................................................ix

About the Technical Reviewer ..........................................................xi

Chapter 1: An Introduction to Regular Expressions............................1

Why Are Regular Expressions Important? ..........................................1

What Are Regular Expressions? ........................................................2

Frustrations with Regular Expressions Arise from Lack of Taking Action ..............4

Regular Expressions Are Imperative ..................................................5

The Language Family of Regular Expressions .....................................6

Summary.........................................................................................8

Chapter 2: Regex Syntax 101 .............................................................9

Formulating an Expression ..............................................................9

Literal Characters and Meta Characters......................................10

Arbitrary Character Class................................................................13

Basic Concatenation ......................................................................14

Alternative Execution .....................................................................14

Operator Precedence and Parentheses............................................15

Anchored Start and End ..................................................................15

Modifiers........................................................................................19

Summary.........................................................................................21

## Chapter 3: Executing Regular Expressions........................................**23**

Regular Expressions in JavaScript...............................................23

RegExp Methods.......................................................25

String Methods Accepting Regular Expressions........................26

Regex Modifiers......................................................27

Global Matches.......................................................28

Multiline Matches....................................................30

ES6 Unicode Regular Expressions......................................31

Sticky Matches.......................................................32

Summary..............................................................34

Other PCRE-Based Regex Environments...............................34

PHP.................................................................35

Python..............................................................37

Perl 5..............................................................40

Java................................................................41

R...................................................................43

C#..................................................................44

Ruby................................................................46

Golang..............................................................48

C++.................................................................49

Summary.............................................................51

## Chapter 4: Visualizing Regex Execution Using Finite State Machines ...............................................................**53**

Regular Expressions Are Finite State Machines.......................53

Backtracking........................................................55

Deterministic and Nondeterministic Regex Modeling..................56

Basic Regex Simplifications.................................................................62

A Successful Match Is Cheaper Than Failure................................63

Automatically Generating Regex FSMs.........................................63

Summary..........................................................................................66

**Chapter 5: Repeat Modifiers ...........................................67**

Backtracking....................................................................................68

Match at Least Once.......................................................................70

Match at Most Once: Optionals.....................................................72

Match Any Number of Times.........................................................73

Fixed-Range Matching....................................................................74

Loop Exactly n Times.....................................................................77

Greedy Repeat Modifiers................................................................78

Lazy Repeat Modifiers....................................................................79

Possessive Repeat Modifiers.........................................................82

Summary..........................................................................................84

**Chapter 6: Character Sets and Character Classes...........85**

Character Sets.................................................................................85

Character Set Ranges.....................................................................87

Exclusions from Character Sets.....................................................88

Character Set Classes.....................................................................88

Concatenating Advanced Language Constructs.............................92

Summary..........................................................................................93

**Chapter 7: Substring Extraction from Regular Expressions ..............95**

Defining Capture Groups................................................................96

Perl 6 Capture Groups....................................................................97

Retrieval of Captured Substrings ................................................................98

    JavaScript..........................................................................................100

    PHP ....................................................................................................101

    Python ................................................................................................102

    Perl 5 .................................................................................................103

Reusing Captured Substrings Within a Regex...........................................104

Capture Groups and Performance..............................................................106

Extensions to Capture Groups....................................................................108

Summary.....................................................................................................108

**Chapter 8: Lookahead and Lookbehind ...............................109**

Lookahead...................................................................................................109

Lookbehind .................................................................................................112

Summary.....................................................................................................113

**Chapter 9: Maintaining Regular Expressions ....................115**

Extended Mode ...........................................................................................116

Regex Subroutines......................................................................................118

    PCRE Subroutines...............................................................................119

    Perl 6 Subroutines..............................................................................120

    Recursion and Circular References with Subroutines..................................121

    Extended Mode, Subroutines, and Abstractions .........................................121

Named Capture Groups...............................................................................122

    EMACS Named Capture Groups...........................................................122

    PCRE Named Capture Groups..............................................................122

    Perl 6 Named Capture Groups .............................................................125

Case Study: XRegExp Library for JavaScript..............................................125

Summary.....................................................................................................128

**Chapter 10: Optimizing Regular Expressions ............................131**

Summary of the Optimization Techniques ........................................132

Making Character Classes More Specific ........................................132

Repeating Character Class Loops .................................................134

Use Possessive Repeat Modifiers Whenever Possible ..........................135

Use Atomic Groups.......................................................................136

Refactor for Optimization .............................................................138

Optimization Techniques Limit Nondeterministic Execution ...................138

Summary....................................................................................139

**Chapter 11: Parsing HTML Code and URL Query Strings
        with Regular Expressions ..............................................141**

Parsing HTML Tags......................................................................141

Processing the Query String of a URL ...........................................144

**Afterword: This Is Not the End, but the Beginning............................147**

"What If I Want to Learn More?" ...................................................149

Keep in Touch.............................................................................150

**Index..................................................................................151**

# About the Author

 **Zsolt Nagy** is a web development team lead, mentor, and software engineer living in Berlin, Germany. He programs with JavaScript, Perl, and other open source web technologies. Zsolt is also experienced in using and teaching regular expressions using these technologies. He writes a blog about lessons learned while solving complex problems, experimenting with technology, and teaching other people how to improve their skills. As a software engineer, he continuously challenges himself to stick to the highest possible standards.

You can read regular articles from me on

- zsoltnagy.eu, a blog on writing maintainable web applications
- devcareermastery.com, a career blog on designing a fulfilling career

Sign up to my e-mail list for regular free content. I am the author of these two books:

- ES6 in Practice: The Complete Developer's Guide (`https://leanpub.com/es6-in-practice`)
- The Developer's Edge: How to Double Your Career Speed with Soft-Skills (`https://leanpub.com/thedevelopersedge`)

Check them out if these topics are interesting to you.

# About the Technical Reviewer

 **Massimo Nardone** has a master of science degree in computing science from the University of Salerno, Italy, and has more than 24 years of experience in the areas of security, web/mobile development, cloud, and IT architecture. His IT passions are security and Android.

Specifically, he has worked as a project manager, software engineer, research engineer, chief security architect, information security manager, PCI/SCADA auditor, and senior lead IT security/cloud/SCADA architect.

He has also worked as a visiting lecturer and supervisor for exercises at the Networking Laboratory of the Helsinki University of Technology (Aalto University), and he holds four international patents (in the PKI, SIP, SAML, and proxy areas).

He currently works as the chief information security officer (CISO) for Cargotec Oyj and is a member of the ISACA Finland Chapter board.

Massimo has reviewed more than 45 IT books for different publishing companies and is the coauthor of *Pro JPA 2 in Java EE 8* (Apress, 2018), *Beginning EJB in Java EE 8* (Apress, 2018), and *Pro Android Games* (Apress, 2015).

# CHAPTER 1

# An Introduction to Regular Expressions

I still remember my doomed encounters with regular expressions back when I tried to learn them. In fact, I took pride in not using regular expressions. I always found a long workaround or a code snippet. I projected and blamed my own lack of expertise on the hard readability of regular expressions. This process continued until I was ready to face the truth: regular expressions are powerful, and they can save you a lot of time and headache.

Fast-forward a couple of years. People I worked with encountered the same problems. Some knew regular expressions, and others hated them. Among the haters of regular expressions, it was quite common that they actually liked the syntax and grammar of their first programming language. Some developers even took courses on formal languages. Therefore, I made it my priority to show everyone a path toward their disowned knowledge to master regular expressions.

## Why Are Regular Expressions Important?

In today's world, we have to deal with processing a lot of data. Accessing data is not the main problem. Filtering data is. Regular expressions provide you with one type of filter that you can use to extract relevant data from

© Zsolt Nagy 2018
Z. Nagy, *Regex Quick Syntax Reference*, https://doi.org/10.1007/978-1-4842-3876-9_1

the big chunks of data available to you. For instance, suppose you have an XML file containing 4GB of data on movies. Regular expressions make it possible to query this XML text so that you can find all movies that were filmed in Budapest in 2016, for instance.

Regular expressions are a must-have for software developers.

In front-end development, we often validate input using regular expressions. Many small features are also easier with regular expressions, such as splitting strings, parsing input, and matching patterns.

When writing backend code, especially in the world of data science, we often search, replace, and process data using regular expressions. In IT infrastructure, regular expressions have many use cases. VIM and EMACS also come with regex support for finding commands, as well as editing text files.

Regular expressions are everywhere. These skills will come handy for you in your IT engineering career.

# What Are Regular Expressions?

Regular expressions, or *regexes*, come from the theory of formal languages. In theory, a *regex* is a finite character sequence defining a search pattern. We often use these search patterns to

- Test whether a string matches a search expression

- Find some characters in a string

- Replace substrings in a string matching a regex

- Process and format user input

- Extract information from server logs, configuration files, and text files

- Validate input in web applications and in the terminal

A typical regular expression task is *matching*. I will now use JavaScript to show you how to test-drive regular expressions because almost everyone has access to a browser. In the browser, you have to open the Developer Tools. In Google Chrome, you can do this by right-clicking a web site and selecting Inspect. Inside the Developer Tools, select the Console tab to enter and evaluate your JavaScript expressions.

Suppose there is a JavaScript regular expression /re/. This expression looks for a pattern inside a string, where there is an r character, followed by an e character. For the sake of simplicity, suppose our strings are case sensitive.

```
const s1 = 'Regex';
const s2 = 'regular expression';
```

In JavaScript, strings have a match method. This method expects a regular expression and returns some data on the first match.

```
> s1.match( /re/ )
null

> s2.match( /re/ )
["re", index: 0, input: "regular expression"]
```

A regular expression is an expression written inside two slash (/) characters. The expression /re/ searches for an r character followed by an e character.

As an analogy, imagine that you loaded a web site in the browser, pressed Ctrl+F or Cmd+F to find a substring inside the web site on the screen, and started typing re. The regular expression /re/ does the same thing inside the specified string, except that the results are case sensitive.

Notice that 'Regex' does not contain the substring 're'. Therefore, there are no matches.

The string `'regular expression'` contains the substring `'re'` twice: once at position 0 and once at position 11. For the sake of determining the match, the JavaScript regular expression engine returns only the first match at index 0 and terminates.

JavaScript allows you to turn the syntax around by testing the regular expression.

```
> /re/.test( s1 )
false

> /re/.test( s2 )
true
```

The return value is a simple Boolean. Most of the time, you do not need anything more, so testing the regular expression is sufficient.

Each programming language has different syntax for built-in regex support. You can either learn them or generate the corresponding regex code using an online generator such as `https://regex101.com/`.[1]

# Frustrations with Regular Expressions Arise from Lack of Taking Action

According to many software developers, regular expressions are

- Hard to understand

- Hard to write

- Hard to modify

- Hard to test

- Hard to debug

---

[1]`https://regex101.com/`

As I mentioned in the introduction of this chapter, lack of understanding often comes with blame. We tend to blame regular expressions for these five problems.

To figure out why this blaming exists, let's discover the journey of a regular developer, no pun intended, with regexes. Many of us default to this journey of discovery when it comes to playing around with something we don't know well. With regular expressions, the task seems too easy: we just have to create a short expression, right? Well, oftentimes, this point of view is very wrong.

Trial and error oftentimes takes more time than getting the pain handled and getting the lack of knowledge cured. Yet, most developers work with trial and error over and over again. After all, why bother learning the complex mechanics of regular expressions if you could simply copy and paste a small snippet? Learning the ins and outs of regular expressions seems to be too hard at first glance anyway.

Therefore, my mission is to show you that

- Learning regular expressions is a lot easier than you thought

- Knowing regular expressions is fun

- Knowing regular expressions is beneficial in many areas of your software developer career

You can still easily master regular expressions to the extent that they will do exactly what you intended them to do. This mastery comes from understanding the right theory and getting a lot of practice.

# Regular Expressions Are Imperative

Regular expressions are widely misunderstood. Whenever you hear that regular expressions are *declarative*, run from that tutorial or blog as far as you can. Regexes are an imperative language. If you want to understand regexes as declarative, chances are you will fail.

By definition, regexes specify a search pattern. Although this is a true statement, it is easy to misinterpret it because you are not specifying a declarative structure. In the real world, you specify a sequence of instructions acting like a function in an imperative programming language. You use commands and loops, you pass arguments to your regex, you may pass arguments around inside your regex, you return a result, and you may even cause side effects.

Learning regular expressions as an imperative language comes with a big advantage. If you have dealt with at least one programming language in your life, chances are, you know almost everything to understand regular expressions. You are just not yet proficient in the regex syntax. As soon as you familiarize yourself with this weird language, everything will fall into place.

# The Language Family of Regular Expressions

When I talk about regular expressions, in practice I mean a family of different dialects. Similarly to genetics, regular expressions keep evolving, and new mutations surface on a regular basis. Although the principles stay the same in most languages, every single dialect brings something different.

Standardization of regular expressions began with *BRE* (Basic Regular Expressions) inside the POSIX standard 1003.2. This standard is used in the editors ed and sed, as well as in the grep command.

The first major evolution of regular expressions came with the *ERE* (Extended Regular Expressions) syntax. This syntax is used in, for example, egrep and notepad++.

For completeness, I will also mention the *SRE* (Simple Regular Expressions) dialect, which has been deprecated in favor of BRE.

Some editors such as EMACS and VIM have their own dialects. In the case of VIM, the dialect can be customized with flags, and this technique provides even more variations. These dialects are built on top of ERE.

The regular expressions used in most programming languages are based on the *PCRE* (Perl Compatible Regular Expressions) dialect. Each programming language has its own abbreviations and differences. These programming languages include PHP, JavaScript, Java, C#, C++, Python, R, Perl up to version 5, and more.

To make matters more complex, Perl 6 comes with a completely different set of rules for regular expressions. The Perl 6 syntax is often easier to read, but in exchange, you have to learn a different language.

As an example, let's write a regex for matching strings that contain at least one non-numeric character.

| Dialect | Expression |
| --- | --- |
| BRE, ERE, EMACS, VIM, PCRE | /[^0123456789]/ |
| Perl 6 | /<-[0123456789]>/ |

As you can see, in this specific example, all dialects but Perl 6 look identical. Without getting lost in the details too much, let's understand what this expression means in BRE, ERE, EMACS, VIM, and PCRE.

- [0123456789] matches one single character from the character set of digits.

- ^ inside an enumeration negates the character list. This means [^0123456789] matches any character that's not a digit.

- As the regular expression may match any character of the test string, a match is determined as soon as you find at least one character in the test string that's not a digit. Therefore, 123.45 matches the regular expression, while 000 does not.

The Perl 6 syntax works in the same way; the syntax is just different.

Let's now write a regular expression that matches the 0, 1, or 2 character, using the or operator of regular expressions.

```
BRE:               or operator is not supported
ERE,PCRE,Perl 6:   /0|1|2/
EMACS,VIM:         /0\|1\|2/
```

An equivalent BRE expression would be /[012]/, using a character set. You will study character sets in detail in Chapter 6.

As studying six groups and many different variations would take a long time, I highly recommend you stick to one specific dialect and practice your skills focusing on the one and only dialect you use in practice. You can come back to study other dialects later. When it comes to the PCRE dialect, different languages give you different variations. I have personally found it beneficial to build and execute regular expressions in multiple programming languages. This way, I had an easier time solidifying my regex knowledge from different angles.

# Summary

In this chapter, I defined a regular expression as a finite character sequence defining a search pattern. As an example, you saw a test execution of a simple JavaScript regular expression in the console. Although the tested regular expression was simple, oftentimes people have a hard time constructing and understanding regular expressions. This is because regular expressions represent a compact imperative language, and therefore, they are often not intuitive to understand. To make matters more complicated, regular expressions consist of multiple languages, which means that the JavaScript syntax is completely different than the syntax used in Perl 6.

# CHAPTER 2

# Regex Syntax 101

When learning a new tool, you always have to get started somewhere.

The goal of this chapter is to give you a basic subset of the regular expression syntax to play with. Learning all the syntax is not productive, though, because let's face it, learning advanced regular expression syntax all at once is too much for anyone.

## Formulating an Expression

A regular expression is written inside a starting slash and an ending slash character: /re/.

As you saw in Chapter 1, this expression matches strings containing re.

Some programming languages allow you or require you to use a different notation. For instance, in JavaScript, you may use the following form to define the regular expression /re/:

```
> const regex = new RegExp( 're' );
> regex
/re/
```

In PHP and Python, you have to use strings or raw strings to pass a regular expression to a function. Here's a Python example:

```
import re

regex = re.compile(r"xy+")
```

© Zsolt Nagy 2018
Z. Nagy, *Regex Quick Syntax Reference*, https://doi.org/10.1007/978-1-4842-3876-9_2

Unless dealing with a specific example in a specific language, I will stick to the /re/ notation in this book.

# Literal Characters and Meta Characters

A regex *literal character* matches itself. The expression /a/ matches any string that contains the a character.

For instance, the expression /a/ matches the string "andrea" because both the first and last letters of the string are a. Matching often comes with simplifications in execution. During execution, the regex engine locates only the first character of the string, which is an a. Given the character matches the expression, you are done; there is no need to read the rest of the string.

The expression /a/ does not match the string "ABCDEA" because after reading the whole string, we did not find a single a character.

All lowercase and uppercase alphabetical characters and all numerical characters are available as literal characters. Depending on the regex dialect, some other characters can also be used to match themselves. For instance, !, %, =, and _ are available in most dialects as literal characters.

Characters such as ., *, ^, $, [, and ] are not literal characters in almost any dialect. They are *meta characters*. A meta character is responsible for denoting an operation similarly to a keyword in a programming language. Table 2-1 describes meta characters.

***Table 2-1.*** *Meta Characters*

| Meta Character | Semantics |
| --- | --- |
| . | Arbitrary character |
| * | Iteration: match any number of times |
| ^ | Two semantics: (1) negation, (2) anchor matching the start of the string or line |
| $ | Anchor matching the end of the string or line |
| [] | Character sets |

In PCRE, the language family of programming languages, even more characters are reserved, as shown in Table 2-2.

***Table 2-2.*** *PCRE Meta Characters*

| PCRE Meta Character | Semantics |
| --- | --- |
| \| | Alternative execution (or) |
| ? | Optional parts in the expression |
| + | Match at least once |
| {} | Specify a range for the number of times an expression has to match the string |
| () | Grouping characters (1), or extracting substrings (2) |

In VIM and EMACS, you have to escape the characters |, ?, {, }, (, and ) to use them as operators.

If you want to use any of the reserved characters, you have to escape them with a backslash.

The treatment of whitespaces is complicated. When searching for patterns in free text, it is rarely convenient to enter the exact whitespace you are looking for. Unfortunately in most dialects, a space matches a space, the \n character matches a newline, and the \t character matches a tab. The problem with this approach is that the exact whitespace characters become important in the search expression.

This approach reminds me of a weird front-end experience of mine. I created a user interface to help users parse CSV files. In the user interface, there was a field for entering the CSV separator character. Once an administrator called me. He showed me that he pasted a tab whitespace character in a text field so that his CSV separator became a tab. Unfortunately, the input field got trimmed, and the tab character could not be saved because the input field had to contain at least one whitespace character.

11

Whitespace characters are often a mess.

You will learn later that you can add flags to the end of a regular expression. These flags may influence how you treat whitespace characters.

In some cases, the input string is split into lines, and regular expressions are expected to match each line. In other cases, input strings may contain newline characters, and these newlines can be matched by the regular expression. This implies that some flags may change the behavior of matching newline characters.

The Perl 6 dialect handles whitespaces completely differently than any other dialect. Perl 6 ignores all whitespace characters in a regular expression, making whitespaces less of a riddle than in other dialects. You will see later that ignoring whitespaces comes with the benefit that you can format regular expressions in any way you want. The following are equivalent when whitespaces don't matter:

```
/first second third/
```

```
/
  first
  second
  third
/
```

A whitespace character in a regular expression matches any sequence of whitespaces in the tested string.

The x, or extended mode, flag of some PCRE regular expressions turns the same formatting mode on. Note that this flag is not available in all PCRE languages.

```
/(?x)
    first
    second
    third
/
```

As a summary, be careful with whitespace anomalies. Avoid using whitespaces in regular expressions. You will soon find out how to handle whitespaces properly, once I introduce named character classes.

# Arbitrary Character Class

In some cases, you will look for an arbitrary character. Creating an enumeration of all possible characters does not really make sense.

In all regular expression dialects, the . symbol denotes one arbitrary character. For instance, /..e/ denotes a three-letter sequence ending with e.

Unfortunately, in different dialects, the . character is defined differently because it may or may not include the newline character.

- Perl 6 follows the command-line regex format defined by BRE and ERE. In other words, a . represents any character, including the newline.

- In all other languages represented by the PCRE language family, a . character represents any character except the newline. Therefore, matching the newline character has to be explicitly specified. EMACS and VIM follow this approach.

For maintainability reasons, it is advised to explicitly specify the type of character you are interested in matching. You will learn how to do this in Chapter 6. Until then, using [.\n] makes sure you include the newline character together with the arbitrary character class.

# Basic Concatenation

In all programming languages, the three necessary control elements are *sequencing, selection,* and *iteration.* Concatenation is responsible for sequencing.

You have already used concatenation in several places. First you used it in Chapter 1 when you defined the /re/ regular expression. You read /re/ as follows: match the character r and *then* match the character e.

When constructing regular expressions, you can concatenate any regular expression sequences.

# Alternative Execution

Now that you know how to do sequencing, let's move on to selection. Let's recall the example from Chapter 1, shown here:

```
BRE:              or operator is not supported
EMACS,VIM:        /0\|1\|2/
ERE,PCRE,Perl 6:  /0|1|2/
```

You have already learned that the | or \| operator specifies alternative paths. /0|1|2/ matches a character that is a 0 *or* a 1 *or* a 2.

Here are some examples:

- /java|php|perl/ matches strings containing java *or* php *or* perl.

- /....|a|the/ matches any string that is at least four characters long *or* contains the character a *or* contains the substring the.

The pipe operator has the lowest precedence out of all the operators in regular expressions.

# Operator Precedence and Parentheses

Concatenation binds stronger than alternative execution. Think of concatenation as if it was multiplication, and think of alternative execution as if it was addition. You do not need any parentheses in /a|the/ because concatenation binds stronger. Similarly, you don't need any parentheses when you calculate 1 + 2 * 3, which is 1 + 6 = 7.

Sometimes you want to override the default precedence rules. This is where parentheses come in handy. You can use parentheses to group expressions with lower precedence.

For instance, the expression /list|lost|lust/ can be simplified to /l(i|o|u)st/. You can use any number of nested parentheses for grouping.

Don't forget to escape the parentheses in VIM and EMACS.

For the sake of completeness, be aware that the usage of parentheses is overloaded. Parentheses will be used to *capture* substrings from regular expressions. You will explore this use case at a later stage.

Parentheses are meta characters that do not consume any characters from the string the regex is testing. There are many other commands that do not cause a traversion inside the string. For instance, in the next section, you will learn about the anchored start and end that do not consume any characters either.

# Anchored Start and End

In some dialects such as JavaScript, the ^ and $ symbols represent the beginning and the end of the string to be matched. In other environments such as in EMACS and VIM, the ^ and $ symbols represent the beginning and the end of the line to be matched.

In BRE, ERE, many PCRE-based languages, and Perl 6,

- /^x/ matches strings that start with x.
- /x$/ matches strings that end with x.
- /^x$/ matches the string 'x' with no other characters present.

In some PCRE-based languages, the previous characters only denote line boundary assertions. For instance, in Ruby,

- /^x/ matches lines that start with x.
- /x$/ matches lines that end with x.
- /\Ax/ matches strings that start with x.
- /x\z/ matches strings that end with x.

Whenever ^ and $ formulate restrictions defined on lines, you use the \A and \z or \Z characters, respectively, for the strings containing all lines in many PCRE-based languages.

This is not a generic rule, because in JavaScript, \A means the literal character A. JavaScript uses the word boundary assertion \b to test for the start or end of a word.

- /\bx/ matches words starting with x.
- /x\b/ matches words ending with x.

Furthermore, in JavaScript, the m multiline modifier redefines ^ and $ to assert the start and end of a line, respectively. You will learn about the multiline modifier in the next chapter.

In EMACS,

- /\`x/ matches strings that start with x.
- /^x/ matches lines that start with x.
- /x\'/ matches strings that end with x.
- /x$/ matches lines that end with x.

16

In VIM,

- /\%^x/ matches strings that start with `x`.

- /^x/ matches lines that start with `x`.

- /x\%$/ matches strings that end with `x`.

- /x$/ matches lines that end with `x`.

In Perl 6,

- `/^x/` matches strings that start with `x`.

- `/x$/` matches strings that end with `x`.

- `/^^x/` matches lines that start with `x`.

- `/x$$/` matches lines that end with `x`.

You can conclude that anchored start and end characters may behave completely differently in different dialects. Always check your documentation and test your work before relying on these assertions.

**Exercise 1**: Which of the following strings does /^list|lost|lust$/ match in JavaScript, and why?

- list,

- lostlist,

- listlist,

- lustlist?

**Solution**: Surprisingly, the answer is, the first three strings match. Here's the proof:

```
> 'list'.match( /^list|lost|lust$/ )
["list", index: 0, input: "list"]

> 'lostlist'.match( /^list|lost|lust$/ )
["lost", index: 0, input: "lostlist"]
```

```
> 'listlist'.match( /^list|lost|lust$/ )
["list", index: 0, input: "listlist"]

> 'lustlist'.match( /^list|lost|lust$/ )
null
```

You may have erroneously thought that the regular expression matches strings `'list'`, `'lost'`, and `'lust'`, and nothing else, because the start and the end of the string are all anchored.

If you expected only `list` to match the regular expression, recall a sentence from the alternative execution section: the pipe operator has the lowest precedence out of all operators in regular expressions.

The | operator has the lowest precedence, which means that both the ^ and the $ bind stronger. If you use parentheses to highlight the natural precedence, you get the following expression:

```
/(^list)|lost|(lust$)/
```

This expression reads as follows: you match any string that

- Either starts with `list`

- Or contains `lost`

- Or ends with `lust`

The second string, `'lostlist'`, matches this expression, because it contains `lost`. The third string, `'listlist'`, matches this expression because it starts with `list`.

The fourth string, `'lustlist'`, does not match this expression because it does not start with `list`, does not contain `lost`, and does not end with `lust`.

If you want to limit your matches to exclusively `list`, `lost`, and `lust`, you have to use parentheses.

```
/^(list|lost|lust)$/
```

After adding parentheses, only the first string matches the expression.

```
> 'list'.match( /^(list|lost|lust)$/ )
["list", index: 0, input: "list"]

> 'lostlist'.match( /^(list|lost|lust)$/ )
null

> 'listlist'.match( /^(list|lost|lust)$/ )
null

> 'lustlist'.match( /^(list|lost|lust)$/ )
null
```

When using anchor characters with |, always denote your intended precedence with parentheses, even if your intentions are obvious to you and even if the usage of parentheses is redundant. This way, your expressions will become more maintainable.

# Modifiers

It is possible to add different modifiers to a regular expression to change the way the expression is interpreted and executed. Modifiers are typically written after the end of the expression.

The bad news is different regular expression implementations come with different modifiers. The good news is before working with a language, you can look up and get used to the modifiers available in your language.

Table 2-3 shows some examples of modifiers.

***Table 2-3.*** *Modifiers*

| Modifier | Semantics |
|----------|-----------|
| g | Global matching, which does not return after the first match. |
| m | Multiline matching to make ^ and $ match the start and end of a line instead of the start and the end of the whole string. |
| s | Single-line mode. The character . matches all characters including \n. |
| i | Case-insensitive matching. |
| x | Ignore whitespace characters. This option turns on free spacing mode. |
| u | Match with full Unicode. |

These flags are not universal. For instance, the x flag is not available in JavaScript. The g flag is not available in PHP because global mode can be accessed only by invoking a different matcher function.

Let's see the effects of case-insensitive mode in the JavaScript console:

```
> /re/.test( 'Regex' );
false

> /re/i.test( 'Regex' );
true
```

Case-insensitive mode treats the string as case insensitive, matching the sequence Re with the regular expression /re/i.

For now, you can assume /re/i and /(r|R)(e|E)/ are equivalent. This is not exactly true because of two reasons affecting efficiency.

- You will later learn a more optimal way of representing character sets representing, for example, a character from the set {r, R}.

- You will learn the secondary function of parentheses used for capturing substrings, which may drastically slow down regular expressions.

Don't worry about performance considerations in this section. Focus on getting the syntax right.

## Summary

This chapter covered some basic building blocks that make it possible for you to understand and construct basic regular expressions.

You learned how to formulate a regular expression, what characters you can use as literal characters, and how to use meta characters.

This chapter also introduced concatenation and alternative execution matching characters after each other or as alternatives.

The . character was introduced as a shorthand for one arbitrary character.

I concluded this chapter with anchoring the start and end of a string or a line and with previewing some modifiers. You will use some of these modifiers in the next chapter, where you will execute PCRE-based regular expressions in many different programming languages.

# CHAPTER 3

# Executing Regular Expressions

Regular expressions can be used in different programming languages and text editors. As it is important to test your code in different environments, in this chapter you will get to know how to construct and execute regexes in your own environment.

Don't worry about memorizing the details in all languages. The goal in this chapter is to explore and play with regexes. You don't have to put pressure on yourself to memorize language elements I have not yet explained in detail. Once you get to the verbose explanation of a feature you may not yet understand, remembering what you have read in this chapter will increase your familiarity with the language construct.

First, you will get to know regular expressions in JavaScript in depth so that you can experiment with regexes in the browser. Then you will get a chance to use some web sites to execute regular expressions in many other programming languages.

Once again, the mind-set of this chapter is "No pressure. Have fun."

## Regular Expressions in JavaScript

It is easy to experiment with JavaScript regular expressions, as JavaScript is accessible in all browsers.

I will use the Chrome Developer Tools to execute regular expressions. The > symbol at the front of each line denotes input. The return value and console logs are printed after the input lines. As we are experimenting in the console, I will use global variables. Obviously, in the source code, using let and const is encouraged.

Regular expressions can be constructed in two ways.

In their literal form, a regex pattern can be written in between slashes (/), and some global modifiers can be added to them in the end.

In their object form, you use the RegExp constructor to create regular expressions. The two forms are identical.

```
> new RegExp( 'xy+' )
/xy+/
```

The xy+ pattern matches strings that contain an x character followed by at least one y character.

JavaScript regular expressions are objects.

```
> typeof /xy+/
"object"
```

The constructor function allows the runtime compilation of the expression. For instance, you could construct a regex pattern using a visual editor, assemble a string based on the visual editor, and pass it to the RegExp constructor as an argument during runtime.

# RegExp Methods

There are many use cases for regular expressions in JavaScript. You can identify these use cases by examining the public interface of regexes, which describe the methods executable on RegExp objects.

- exec executes a search returning information on a match.

- test executes a search returning a Boolean indicating whether a match was found.

- toString stringifies a regular expression.

```
> /xy+/.exec( 'yyxyy' );
{0: "xyy", index: 2, input: "yyxyy", length: 1}

> /xy+/.test( 'yyxyy' );
true

> /xy+/.toString()
"/xy+/"
```

Notice that exec returns the *longest* match xyy, not the shortest match xy. This is because the y+ construct acts like a loop that matches as many y characters as it finds. In other words, the y+ construct is greedy. You will learn about the behavior of the + meta character in Chapter 5.

Notice in the previous test example that from the point of view of finding a match, the xy+ search expression is equivalent to using xy. This is because locating *one* y character implies that you can also locate *at least one*.

Therefore, in the method test, /xy+/ and /xy/ behave in the same way. In other methods, y+ finds the longest sequence of y characters.

# String Methods Accepting Regular Expressions

Some string methods accept regular expressions as arguments.

- match executes a search in the string returning information on the upcoming match. It's like the exec method on RegExp objects, exchanging the object and the argument.

- search executes a search in the string returning the index of the upcoming match. The returned index is -1 if the regex pattern cannot be found in the string.

- replace executes a search in the string and replaces the first match.

- split splits a string into substrings based on a specified regex pattern.

Here are some examples:

```
> s = 'xyyzxyzz';
> s.match( /xy+/ );
{ 0: "xyy", index: 0, input: "xyyzxyzz", length: 1 }

> s.search( /xy+/ );
0

> s.replace( /xy+/, 'U' )
"Uzxyzz"

> s
"xyyzxyzz"

> s.split( /xy+/ )
["", "z", "zz"]
```

Notice that `replace` does not mutate the original string; it just returns a new string with the replaced values.

The `split` method of strings is polymorphic in a sense that it accepts a string as well as a regular expression. In the latter case, the string split is made according to the longest possible matches.

# Regex Modifiers

The second argument of the `RegExp` constructor function is the list of flags applied to the regular expression. These flags are called *modifiers*. For instance, for a case-sensitive search, you can apply the `i` flag.

```
> x = new RegExp( 'x' )
/x/

> xX = new RegExp( 'x', 'i' )
/x/i

> x.test( 'XY' )
false

> xX.test( 'XY' )
true
```

Table 3-1 describes the modifiers available in JavaScript.

***Table 3-1.*** *JavaScript Modifiers*

| Modifier | Description |
| --- | --- |
| i | Non-case-sensitive matching. Uppercase and lowercase don't matter. |
| g | Global match. You attempt to find all matches instead of just returning the first match. The internal state of the regular expression stores where the last match was located, and matching is resumed where it was left in the previous match. |
| m | Multiline match. It treats the ^ and $ characters to match the beginning and the end of each line of the tested string. A newline character is determined by \n or \r. |
| u | Unicode search. The regex pattern is treated as a Unicode sequence. |
| y | Sticky search. |
| s | Single-line matching. The . character will also match newline characters such as \r and \n. Available in ES2018 and newer. |

Single-line matching is a construct that was added to the regex engine of JavaScript with ES2018. I will not cover this flag in this chapter. Let's execute a few examples for the rest of the flags.

# Global Matches

Let's construct an example for global matching. We will find all the sequences of x characters.

```
> regex = /x+/g;
> str = 'yxxxyxyxx';
> regex.exec( str )
```

```
{0: 'xxx', index: 1, input: 'yxxxyxyxx' }

> regex.lastIndex
4

> regex.exec( str )
{ 0: "x", index: 5, input: "yxxxyxyxx" }

> regex.exec( str )
{ 0: "xx", index: 7, input: "yxxxyxyxx" }

> regex.exec( str )
null

> str.match( /x+/ )
{0: 'xxx', index: 1, input: 'yxxxyxyxx' }

> str.match( /x+/g )
["xxx", "x", "xx"]
```

In the exec example, you can see that all three matches are returned one by one. After the third match, `null` is returned. The `lastIndex` property of the global regular expression stores the position where it needs to resume execution.

You have already learned that with string matching, the return value is similar to the first execution of `regex.exec`. However, with a global regex argument, the return value is an array containing *all* matches in sequential order.

# Multiline Matches

Let's execute a multiline example. The regular expression

```
> xRow = /^x+$/m
```

defines that each row of a possibly multiline string can contain only lowercase x characters, and each row has to contain at least one x character. The ^ character indicates that each row has to start with the specified regex sequence. The $ character indicates that each row has to end with the specified regex sequence.

The match function specifies that the first row of the string matches all the specified criteria.

```
'xx\nxXx\nxxxx'.match( xRow )
["xx", index: 0, input: "xxxXxxxxx"]
```

If you want to retrieve all matches, you have to add the global flag to the regular expression. This expression matches the first and third rows of the string, ignoring the second row:

```
'xx\nxXx\nxxxx'.match( /^x+$/mg )
["xx", "xxxx"]
```

Without the flags, the newline characters count as whitespace. As whitespace characters are not equal to x, the string does not match the regular expression.

```
'xx\nxXx\nxxxx'.match( /^x+$/ )
null
```

As you can see, without the multiline flag, the ^ and $ characters indicate that the whole string may only contain characters specified by the pattern x+.

# ES6 Unicode Regular Expressions

In ES6, you can specify Unicode characters for matching. A Unicode
character is treated as one character regardless of the number of bytes the
character occupies.

```
> 'x'.codePointAt( 0 ).toString( 16 )
"78"
```

The hexadecimal code of the x character is 78. The corresponding
Unicode character in JavaScript is \u{78}. However, a regular expression
containing this Unicode character does not match the character itself.

```
> /\u{78}/.test( 'x' )
false
```

This is why you need the u flag.

```
> /\u{78}/u.test( 'x' )
true
```

Another problem with Unicode characters is that their size in bytes
may vary. For instance, '\u{2ABCD}' is a Unicode character that cannot be
represented using 4 bytes.

Let's construct a regular expression that checks whether the
corresponding string contains exactly one character. You can do this
using the arbitrary character symbol .. You can specify that your string
starts with this character, ends with this character, and has nothing in
between: /^.$/.

Let's test under what conditions does the string '\u{2ABCD}' match
this regex: /^.$/. As this book is not able to handle long Unicode
characters, I will give you both a screenshot (see Figure 3-1) and the code.
The Unicode character will be a rectangle in the code.

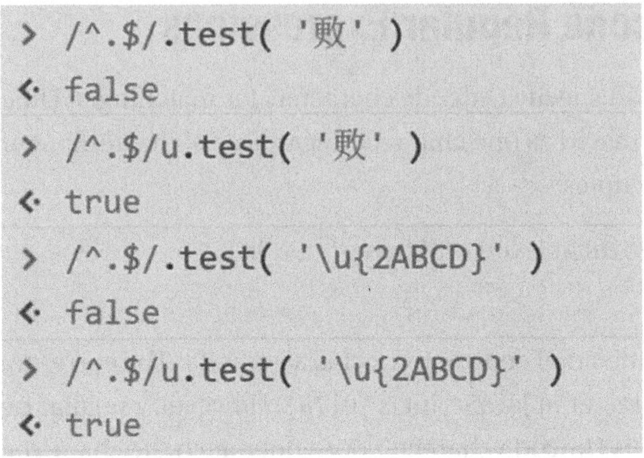

```
> /^.$/.test( '敷' )
< false
> /^.$/u.test( '敷' )
< true
> /^.$/.test( '\u{2ABCD}' )
< false
> /^.$/u.test( '\u{2ABCD}' )
< true
```

*Figure 3-1.* *Unicode flag for JavaScript regular expressions*

```
> /^.$/.test( '[]' )
false

> /^.$/u.test( '[]' )
true

> /^.$/.test( '\u{2ABCD}' )
false

> /^.$/u.test( '\u{2ABCD}' )
true
```

We can conclude that the old JavaScript regex engine interprets `'\u{2ABCD}'` as a sequence of two characters. However, with the u flag, the long Unicode character is recognized as a single character.

# Sticky Matches

The y flag sets the `lastIndex` property of a regular expression after a match to the first character after the last matched sequence. If the last execution of the regular expression resulted in no matches, `lastIndex` is set to 0.

This is a mutation of the internal state of the regular expression. Always be aware of this side effect! When the y flag is on, a ^ is automatically added to the beginning of the regular expression. This means the character at position lastIndex has to match the start of the regular expression.

Here's an example:

```
> regExp = /ab+/y
/ab+/y

> 'ababbabbb'.match( regExp )
{ 0:"ab", index: 0, input: "ababbabbb" }

> regExp.lastIndex
2

> 'ababbabbb'.match( regExp )
{ 0: "abb", index: 2, input: "ababbabbb" }

> regExp.lastIndex
5

> 'ababbabbb'.match( regExp )
{ 0:"abbb", index: 5, input: "ababbabbb" }

> regExp.lastIndex
9

> 'ababbabbb'.match( regExp )
null

> regExp.lastIndex
0

> 'ababbabbb'.match( regExp )
{ 0: "ab", index: 0, input: "ababbabbb" }

> regExp.lastIndex
2

// ...
```

# Summary

Regular expressions in JavaScript have some unique features worth experimenting with. Some of these features are unique in the JavaScript regular expression virtual machine. Other features are common to other languages.

I didn't focus on the exact syntax of the regex patterns here because you will learn the exact rules at a later stage. Some characters, such as the + (at least once) meta character, act as foreshadowing for the capabilities of regular expressions in most languages.

You learned that regular expressions are objects in JavaScript, and they are integrated into some `String` methods as well.

The `RegExp` public interface allows testing a string, finding the first match, finding all matches, replacing substrings, and even splitting strings.

To perform some of these use cases, you can use some modifiers such as the global `g` modifier, the sticky `y` modifier, or the multiline `m` modifier.

Two more modifiers make it more convenient to process strings: `i` makes the string insensitive to uppercase or lowercase, while `u` makes the JavaScript regex virtual machine handle Unicode characters properly.

# Other PCRE-Based Regex Environments

JavaScript regular expressions are based on the PCRE dialect as well as the regex execution environments of most programming languages. We will now explore how to execute regular expressions in some of the most popular languages.

Given that in the case of most languages executing regular expressions is not as easy as in JavaScript, we will use some tools that make it possible to execute and test regular expressions in the browser.

When you want a quick solution for generating code for matching regular expressions, head over to the code generator of `regex101.com`.[1]

# PHP

PHP offers global functions to handle regular expressions. These start with the following:

- `preg_` matching the Perl PCRE syntax

- `ereg_` based on the ERE dialect

- `mb_ereg` also based on the ERE dialect, with the ability to handle Unicode characters

We will deal only with the PCRE syntax here.

In PHP, some modifiers are the same as in JavaScript, while others are different.

- `i` stands for case-insensitivity just like in JavaScript.

- `m` stands for multiline just like in JavaScript.

- `u` stands for Unicode matching just like in JavaScript.

- `s` makes the `.` character match all characters without exception, including the newline, just like in ES2018.

- `x` turns on free spacing mode for easier readability. Free spacing mode ignores whitespace characters between regex characters.

Consult the PCRE section of the PHP manual[2] for the documentation of all PCRE regex functions.

---

[1]`https://regex101.com/`
[2]`http://php.net/manual/en/ref.pcre.php`

You can execute PHP code online using many sandbox solutions such as writephponline.com[3] or the Joodle PHP online editor.[4]

You can use preg_match to return the first match from a string.

```
preg_match('/xy+/', 'xyxyyxyyy', $matches, PREG_OFFSET_
CAPTURE);
print_r($matches);
```

The result is as follows:

**Array** ( [0] => **Array** ( [0] => xy [1] => 0 ) )

This is an array containing one element describing the match. The match descriptor is an array, where element 0 contains the matched sequence, and the element at index 1 contains the index of the first character of the match.

preg_match_all returns all matches, so it is similar to the g flag in JavaScript. Remember, PHP does not have the g modifier, so global matching is encoded in the public interface in the PCRE regular expression wrapper.

```
preg_match_all('/xy+/', 'xyxyyxyyy', $matches, PREG_OFFSET_
CAPTURE);
print_r($matches);
```

The result contains all matches.

```
Array (
    [0] => Array (
        [0] => Array ( [0] => xy    [1] => 0 )
        [1] => Array ( [0] => xyy   [1] => 2 )
        [2] => Array ( [0] => xyyy  [1] => 5 )
    )
)
```

---

[3]www.writephponline.com/
[4]https://www.jdoodle.com/php-online-editor

Although the preg_ functions act as a wrapper for Perl 5–style regular expressions, there are some small differences in the Perl syntax. Consult the php.net documentation on PCRE pattern differences[5] for more details.

# Python

We will now use python.org's shell[6] to start getting familiar with regular expressions in Python. The re Python module gives you support for PCRE-style regular expressions. You can import this module with import re.

```
>>> import re
```

The compile method of the re module compiles a regular expression based on the pattern string provided to it. You can already assemble many pattern strings using your PCRE knowledge.

```
>>> regex = re.compile(r"xy+")
```

Notice the r in front of the string. In Python, this denotes a raw string. Although in the previous example you can omit this r, in generic cases, you can save a lot of character escaping if you use raw strings.

The search method of a compiled regular expression searches its string argument for a match.

```
>>> regex.search( "QxyxyyQ" )
<_sre.SRE_Match object; span=(1, 3), match='xy'>
```

You can get more information on the result with some methods.

```
>>> result = regex.search( "QxyyxyQ" )

>>> result.group(), result.start(), result.end(), result.span()
('xyy', 1, 4, (1, 4))
```

---

[5]http://php.net/manual/en/reference.pcre.pattern.differences.php
[6]https://www.python.org/shell/

The method group returns the first match in its longest form. The first character of the match and the first character after the match can be retrieved using the start, end, and span methods.

The match method of compiled regular expressions is misleading because it looks for a match from the *start* of the string.

```
>>> regex.match( "QxyxyyQ" )
None
```

```
>>> regex.match( "xyxyyQ" )
<_sre.SRE_Match object; span=(0, 2), match='xy'>
```

Technically, match is redundant because you could use the ^ character to match the start of the string.

```
>>> re.compile( "^xy+" ).search( "xyxyyQ" )
<_sre.SRE_Match object; span=(0, 2), match='xy'>
```

I explained the match method so you would avoid confusing it with search.

There is no need to compile regular expressions because the match and search methods are also available via the re module as a function accepting a regex string and a regular string.

```
>>> re.search( '^xy+', 'xyyyyxyQ' )
<_sre.SRE_Match object; span=(0, 5), match='xyyyy'>
```

It is also possible to enumerate all matches belonging to a search expression. The methods findall and finditer do the trick.

```
>>> re.findall( 'xy+', 'QxyxyyQxyyyQ' )
['xy', 'xyy', 'xyyy']
>>> iterator = re.finditer( 'xy+', 'QxyxyyQxyyyQ' )
>>> for matchNum, match in enumerate(iterator):
...      print ( match.group(), match.span() )
```

```
...
xy (1, 3)
xyy (3, 6)
xyyy (7, 11)
```

In the first example, we enumerated all matches in an array. In the second example, we created an iterator and started iterating on it to print the results one by one.

Now you know enough to understand the example code generated by regex101.com.[7]

```python
import re

regex = r"ab+"

test_str = "ababb"

matches = re.finditer(regex, test_str)

for matchNum, match in enumerate(matches):
    matchNum = matchNum + 1

    print ("Match {matchNum} was found at {start}-{end}: {match}"
        .format(
            matchNum = matchNum,
            start = match.start(),
            end = match.end(),
            match = match.group()
        )
    )
```

---

[7]https://regex101.com/

```
for groupNum in range(0, len(match.groups())):
    groupNum = groupNum + 1

    print ("Group {groupNum} found at {start}-{end}: {group}"
        .format(
            groupNum = groupNum,
            start = match.start(groupNum),
            end = match.end(groupNum),
            group = match.group(groupNum)
        )
    )
```

Note that I formatted the long lines in the code. As the width of this book is limited, this change makes sense, and it is not a good idea to write very long lines of code anyway.

The code sequence prints out the following:

```
Match 1 was found at 0-2: ab
Match 2 was found at 2-5: abb
```

The inner loop of groups was not executed in this example. You will come back to this code later when studying the extraction of substrings using capture groups.

For more information, consult the Python regex documentation.[8]

# Perl 5

The Perl 5 documentation[9] gives you information on how to formulate regular expressions. In this section, you will learn how to execute one simple regular expression and print out some information on the match.

---

[8]https://docs.python.org/2/howto/regex.html
[9]https://perldoc.perl.org/perlre.html

You can execute the code snippets in an online Perl compiler such as the one on rextester.com.[10] A simple match can be executed using the =~ operator.

```
if ( "ababb" =~ /ab+/ ) {
    print "Match";
}
```

The value of "ababb" =~ /ab+/ is 1 whenever the match is successful, 0 otherwise. You can also retrieve the matched string and the string before and after the match.

```
if ( "ababb" =~ /ab+/ ) {
    print "Match: ", $`, "|-->|", $&, "|<--|", $';
}

# Output:
# |-->|ab|<--|abb
```

The g global modifier is available in Perl to retrieve all matches.

```
while ( "ababb" =~ /ab+/g ) {
    print "Match: ", $`, "|-->|", $&, "|<--|", $', '\n';
}

# Output:
# |-->|ab|<--|abb
# ab|-->|abb|<--|
```

# Java

You will now see how to write a simple Java class that can execute some regular expression matching.

---

[10]http://rextester.com/l/perl_online_compiler

If you don't want to install the Java development environment on your machine, you can run Java code using tio.run[11] or compilejava.net.[12]

Let's see the source code first:

```java
import java.util.regex.Matcher;
import java.util.regex.Pattern;

public class Main {
    public static void main( String args[] ) {
        final String regex = "xy+";
        final String string = "QxyxyyQxyyyQ";

        final Pattern pattern = Pattern.compile(regex);
        final Matcher matcher = pattern.matcher(string);

        while (matcher.find()) {
            System.out.println(
                "Full match: " + matcher.group() + "(" +
                matcher.start() + "," + matcher.end() + ")"
            );
        }
    }
}
```

- java.util.regex contains a Matcher and a Pattern utility. Pattern compiles a regular expression, and Matcher creates an object to match a pattern with a string.

- You can iterate on the matcher object using its find method to locate the upcoming target.

---

[11]https://tio.run/#java-openjdk9
[12]https://www.compilejava.net/

   –   The details of the match can be accessed through the matcher object. The getter functions group(), start(), and end() return the matched string, the start index of the match, and the index of the first character after the match, respectively.

The result of the execution is as follows:

```
Full match: xy(1,3)
Full match: xyy(3,6)
Full match: xyyy(7,11)
```

# R

In the R language, using regular expressions is quite straightforward.

You can use the grep function to filter the list of strings according to the regular expression matching it. value = TRUE means that you are interested in the filtered string values. FALSE means you are interested in the indices of the returned values.

```
grep("ab+", strings, value = TRUE)
grep("^ab+", strings, value = TRUE)
grep("ab+", strings, value = FALSE)
grep("^ab+", strings, value = FALSE)
```

Let's create a couple of strings.

```
(strings <- c("XabbbbX", "abb", "aaa", "a", "Abbb", "XabX"))
```

The returned values are as follows:

```
[1] "XabbbbX" "abb" "XabX"
[1] "abb"
[1] 1 2 6
[1] 2
```

The function `regexpr` gives more information about the matches, as shown here:

```
regexpr("ab+", strings)
[1] 2 1 -1 -1 -1 2
attr(,"match.length")
[1] 5 3 -1 -1 -1 2
```

The first line contains the indices of the first matched character in each string.

You could also use `regmatches` to display the matched substrings. First you have to save the matches in a constant and then use this constant as the second argument of the `regmatches` function.

```
matches <- regexpr("ab+", strings)
regmatches( strings, matches )
```

The return value is as follows:

```
[1] "abbbb" "abb" "ab"
```

For more information, consult the R manual.[13]

# C#

The generated C# code of regex101.com[14] executes smoothly and shows how easy it is to use regular expressions in C#.

`System.Text.RegularExpressions` gives you regex support.

Similarly to Java, you have to create a class and a static `Main` function as the entry point of the application.

---

[13]https://stat.ethz.ch/R-manual/R-devel/library/base/html/regex.html
[14]https://regex101.com/

In the `Main` function, you have to define a pattern and a string. Regex101 defined these in the variables `pattern` and `input`, respectively. `Regex.Matches` enumerates all matches for you one by one. Each match is stored in an object of type `Match`. A `Match` object has a `Value` and an `Index` field.

```
using System;
using System.Text.RegularExpressions;

public class Example
{
    public static void Main()
    {
        string pattern = @"ab+";
        string input = @"ababb";

        foreach (Match m in Regex.Matches(input, pattern))
        {
            Console.WriteLine("'{0}' found at index {1}.",
            m.Value, m.Index);
        }
    }
}
```

After executing this code in dotnetfiddle.net,[15] for example, the following text is written to the console:

```
'xy' found at index 0.
'xyy' found at index 2.
```

---

[15]https://dotnetfiddle.net/

# Ruby

Let's test-drive the basics of Ruby regular expressions in an online Ruby console such as repl.it.[16]

```
> /ab+/ =~ 'XabbabX'
=> 1
```

Regex matching is done using the =~ operator. The return value of a regex matching is the first character of the match. When there is no match, nil is returned.

```
> /ab+/ =~ 'XX'
=> nil
```

You can also use the match method of regular expressions. The return value of a match is a MatchData object containing the first match.

```
> /ab+/.match( 'XabbabX' )
=> #<MatchData "abb">
```

You can get the matched string by querying $&.

```
> $&
=> "abb"
```

Let's execute the match once more and access some more data on the matched result.

```
> result = /ab+/.match( 'XabbabX' )
=> #<MatchData "abb">
> result[0]
=> "abb"
> result.pre_match
```

---

```
=> "X"
 > result.post_match
=> "abX"
```

If you are interested in an array of all matches, you can use the scan method of strings.

```
 > 'XabbabX'.scan( /ab+/ )
=> ["abb", "ab"]
```

Similarly to the C# code, the Ruby code generated by regex101.com[17] is also straightforward to interpret.

```
re = /xy+/
str = 'xyxxyyy'

# Print the match result
str.scan(re) do |match|
    puts match.to_s
end
```

- re contains the regular expression, while str is the string you attempt to match.

- By using the str.scan method, you get an array. You can iterate on the array and print all matches.

Check out the Ruby Regular Expression documentation[18] if you are interested in learning more about Ruby regexes.

---

[17]https://regex101.com/
[18]http://ruby-doc.org/core-2.2.0/Regexp.html

# Golang

Use the Go Playground[19] to execute Golang code.

Let's generate some regex tester code using regex101.com.[20]

```go
package main

import (
    "regexp"
    "fmt"
)

func main() {
    var re = regexp.MustCompile(`ab+`)
    var str = `ababb`

    for i, match := range re.FindAllString(str, -1) {
        fmt.Println(match, "found at index", i)
    }
}
```

In the code, we created the regular expression ab+ and the string ababb.

The regex method FindAllStrings finds all substrings matching the regular expression. We can then print out the matched substring as well as its index.

We can use some other Golang features to match regular expressions.

```go
package main

import (
    "regexp"
    "fmt"
)
```

---

[19]https://play.golang.org/
[20]https://regex101.com

```go
func main() {
    var re = regexp.MustCompile(`ab+`)
    var str = `ababb`

    // re.MatchString returns a boolean indicating if there is
    a match
    fmt.Println( re.MatchString(str) )

    // re.FindString returns a string containing the first match
    fmt.Println( re.FindString(str) )

    // re.FindAllString collects all matches in an array
    // Important: FindAllString is written in singular
    fmt.Println( re.FindAllString(str, -1) )
}
```

The Golang Regexp Documentation[21] contains more information on the regexp package.

# C++

The last example is C++. First, for simplicity, you need an online C++ compiler. You can use either onlinegdb.com[22] or cpp.sh.[23]

Let's see a simple regex matching:

```cpp
#include <iostream>
#include <regex>

using namespace std;

int main()
```

---

[21]https://golang.org/pkg/regexp/
[22]https://www.onlinegdb.com/online_c++_compiler
[23]http://cpp.sh/

```
{
    regex r( "ab+" );
    cout << regex_search( "XabbabX", r );

    return 0;
}
```

We can define a regular expression using regex r( regexString ). We can then use the r variable in the regex_search function accepting a string and a regular expression. The return value of regex_search is 1 if a match was found, 0 otherwise.

If you are interested in getting all matches one by one, you need to use an sregex_iterator. This iterator is defined over a string and a regular expression, and it emits the matches one by one.

```
#include <iostream>
#include <regex>

using namespace std;

int main()
{
    regex r( "ab+" );
    string str = "XabbabX";
    sregex_iterator iter(str.begin(), str.end(), r),
                    iter_end;

    smatch nextMatch;

    for ( ;iter != iter_end; ++iter ) {
        cout << (*iter).str() << "\n";
    }

    return 0;
}
```

At each point in time, `iter` points at a regex match. `*iter` gives you the contents at the location specified by `iter`. You can get the matched token itself via the `str()` getter method.

As you can see, you need to know quite a lot of C++ to interpret regular expressions. If you don't know C++, you can still execute your regular expressions using these code snippets. If you do know C++, this code will be a piece of cake for you.

## Summary

Although this chapter just scratched the surface, you can see that in most programming languages, regular expressions are easy to execute. Although the exact specifications vary, they are similar in nature. I highly recommend playing around with them so that you get a feel for how you can execute regexes in languages other than your own programming language.

# CHAPTER 4

# Visualizing Regex Execution Using Finite State Machines

A regular expression is converted into code executed in a virtual machine. This virtual machine runs on the virtual machine of the host language or editor.

Abstract models are helpful for understanding how regular expressions are executed. Although these models often neglect optimization techniques implemented by regex engines, they still give you valuable information on how regexes work.

## Regular Expressions Are Finite State Machines

The easiest way to visualize a regular expression is with a finite state machine.[1] A finite state machine (FSM) is a directed acyclic graph[2] with a

---

[1]https://en.wikipedia.org/wiki/Finite-state_machine
[2]https://en.wikipedia.org/wiki/Directed_acyclic_graph

Z. Nagy, *Regex Quick Syntax Reference*, https://doi.org/10.1007/978-1-4842-3876-9_4

dedicated initial state and a dedicated end state. The FSM representation of a regular expression is as follows:

- The edges (arrows) represent characters we read from the input stream.

- The nodes represent an internal state of the regular expression.

For instance, the regular expression /ab/ can be represented with the finite state machine shown in Figure 4-1.

*Figure 4-1.* /ab/

/ab/ first matches the character a and then the character b. Imagine we are reading the text aabc and want to figure out if this string matches the regular expression /ab/.

Let's place a token on the start node.

1. After reading the first a character, we move the token through the arrow denoted by the a state. The token is now in the intermediate state.

2. After reading the second a, there is no arrow starting in the intermediate state; therefore, we move back to the start state. In this state, we try reading a again. As there is an a arrow originating from the start state, we move to the intermediate state again.

3.  After reading the b character, we move our token
    from the intermediate state to the match state.
    Given that we have reached the match state, the
    string *matches* the regular expression.

Notice the match has been determined without reading the last character in the sequence.

Each character in the regular expression is an instruction executed in sequence. These instructions are matching tasks. Our goal is to reach the match node in any way possible. From the perspective of determining a match, it does not matter how many times we reach the match state, as long as we reach it at least once.

# Backtracking

In some cases, we are stuck in an intermediate node of the finite state automaton. To avoid getting stuck, we are entitled to continue execution by using *backtracking*. Backtracking happens once you fail to reach the match node, and you cannot move anywhere from a node.

*When we backtrack in a finite state automaton, we move backward on the edges until we reach a node that has forward edges that we haven't tried yet.* If you have ever read a Fighting Fantasy gamebook, where you explore the Deathtrap Dungeon, for instance, you might remember how you backtracked from one path of the maze to another. The same thing happens in a regular expression.

As you move forward, you mark the edges you have visited. As you move back, you only try edges that you haven't marked before.

While moving backward on an edge, we also move back our caret pointing at the upcoming character of the input string, *unreading* the character on the edge.

One special form of backtracking is when we move back to the starting node. In this case, we have another move in our arsenal: moving a character forward in the input string and attempting to start a new match.

For instance, when matching the string "abaa" with the regex /aa/, we first read the character a. Then we backtrack because we cannot move forward after the first character. After backtracking, we move the caret forward, leaving the string "baa" to match against /aa/. As we cannot match the character b against a, we move the caret forward again. We now have the string "aa" to match against /aa/. This matching will obviously succeed without any further backtracking.

To understand backtracking more deeply, let's explore the differences between deterministic and nondeterministic regular expression modeling.

# Deterministic and Nondeterministic Regex Modeling

The | (pipe) represents an *or* operation in most regular expression dialects. In EMACS and VIM, you have to escape the pipe, resulting in the \| operator. In BRE, *or* is not supported. In all other dialects, the *or* operator is a regular pipe. In this chapter, we will stick to the latter notation.

/a|b/ is a regular expression that matches either an a character or a b character. The finite state machine representation of this regular expression looks like Figure 4-2.

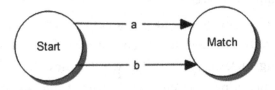

***Figure 4-2.*** /a|b/

In practice, regex implementations may simplify this automaton by representing a set of possible matches using a bitmask, as shown in Figure 4-3.

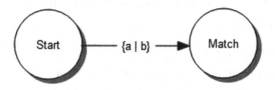

***Figure 4-3.*** */a\b/*

The bitmask representation simplifies the graph, especially in complex cases.

Let's consider some more complex cases, where simplification is not obvious.

Here's an expression, shown in Figure 4-4: /list|lost|lust/.

The most obvious construction of an automaton looks like the following: we branch off for each operand of the *or* operator and attempt to match the characters in sequence.

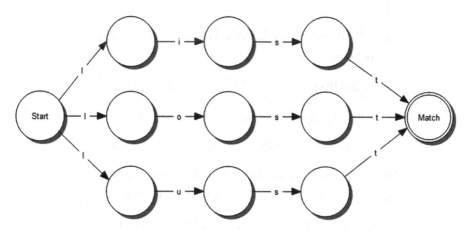

***Figure 4-4.*** */list\lost\lust/*

During execution, we have to attempt each branch. When one branch fails, we backtrack. For instance, in the sequence `lossless`, we attempt the following steps:

- As the first character is `l`, we try to match it in all three branches.

  - On the first branch, we check the second character, which is an `o`. As we cannot move forward in this branch, we backtrack.

  - On the second branch, the second and third characters, `o` and `s`, both match the characters on the upcoming arrows. However, the fourth character is supposed to be a `t` instead of an `s`, so we backtrack.

  - On the third branch, we check the second character, which is still an `o`. As we needed an `u` to move forward, we backtrack.

- The second, third, and fourth characters don't match any of the arrows originating from the *start* node.

- The fifth character is a `l` again. We try to match it in all three branches.

  - On the first branch, `e != i`, so we backtrack.

  - On the second branch, `e != o`, so we backtrack.

  - On the third branch, `e != u`, so we backtrack.

- The rest of the characters (`e`, `s`, and `s`) don't match any of the edges originating from the start node.

- As there are no more letters to read and we have not reached the *match* state, we return a failure.

Each time we can move in multiple directions from the same node, we take a nondeterministic action. The previous automaton is a *nondeterministic finite automaton* (NFA[3]).

Many regex interpreters use this nondeterministic form, without considering any compile-time optimizations. Some regex interpreters go the extra mile and convert the nondeterministic edges into deterministic ones.

First, notice each branch starts with l. We can simply use just one edge instead of the three and delay the nondeterminism, as shown in Figure 4-5.

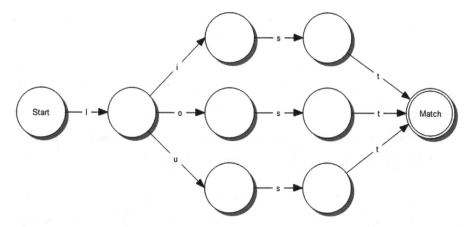

***Figure 4-5.*** */l(ist|ost|ust)/*

---

[3]https://en.wikipedia.org/wiki/Nondeterministic_finite_automaton

Second, notice each branch ends with st. We can use one edge and one state instead of the three redundant ones, as shown in Figure 4-6.

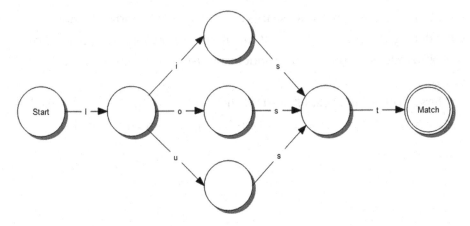

***Figure 4-6.*** *l, I, or o or u, s, t*

As a final step, let's apply a bitmask instead of the three edges, where the letters are connected with *or*, as shown in Figure 4-7.

***Figure 4-7.*** *l, {i, o, u} character set, s, t*

For now, we will denote this bitmask by {i|o|u}. Read it this way: "Choose one of the characters i, o, u." You will learn about this language construct later in the chapter.

More important, the resulting graph is now a DFA,[4] or deterministic finite automaton.

---

[4]https://en.wikipedia.org/wiki/Deterministic_finite_automaton

The nondeterministic form is a lot easier to build from the regular expression. If the length of the input is N, it takes O(N) steps to construct the tree. In exchange, we pay the price during execution, as the worst-case execution time is O(2^N).

Constructing a deterministic automaton takes the magnitude of steps O(2^N). In exchange, execution costs are linear.

In practice, as long as our regular expressions are not reusable, we tend to settle for slower worst-case execution time. This is because a regular expression can succeed very quickly. As soon as we find a match, execution is finished.

Therefore, even though most regex engines use optimizations, the nondeterministic form is often beneficial.

Finally, notice that our original expression was /list|lost|lust/. If we reverse engineer a regular expression from the final optimized automaton, we get /l(i|o|u)st/. This form is purely deterministic. Therefore, we can conclude that in case our regex interpreter has a tendency to execute regex matching in a nondeterministic way, we save precious runtime by writing an optimized regular expression. Even if the interpreter makes the necessary optimizations for us, we still save automaton construction time by writing regexes in an optimized form.

This benefit is often negligible, so whenever we can choose between optimization and understandability, I go for understandability.

If you are interested in learning more about optimization techniques, refer to swtch.com.[5]

---

[5]https://swtch.com/~rsc/regexp/regexp1.html

# Basic Regex Simplifications

You have seen that a nondeterministic automaton construction algorithm yields two completely different automata for the same regular expression. In the previous section,

- /list|lost|lust/ resulted in a nondeterministic finite state automaton.

- /l(i|o|u)st/ resulted in a deterministic one.

You already know that the second form is more efficient. Generally, unless there is a semantic reason to increase the readability of the regular expression, I prefer the second form.

The same holds for constructs, when matching one branch implies that the other branch is matched. For instance, in /lesson|less/ or /less|lesson/, matching lesson implies that we had to match less.

This is because lesson starts with less. As a consequence, we can simplify the regular expression to /less/.

For instance, when executing /lesson|less/ on lessom, which is a nonsense word written most likely as a result of a typo, we first try to match against lesson and then backtrack just to conclude that less is accepted. Although in small regular expressions this is not a big deal, imagine a bloated regular expression like the following:

/less(a|b|c|de(f|g)|o(a|b|c|...))|less/

When checking lessom, we may waste a lot of precious execution time in the first branch for no reason.

We may succeed in the first branch, for instance, by checking the input lessdeg. However, lessdeg also matches less, which means we did unnecessary work. Regular expressions are not designed to find the shortest match. They are designed to return the first match in the execution sequence.

# A Successful Match Is Cheaper Than Failure

You saw in the previous sections that regular expressions tend to succeed faster than returning a failure. This is because a failure means we have to try each execution path in all possible ways.

As success is cheaper than failure, always formulate a condition for success when designing a regular expression. Failure tends to be more expensive.

# Automatically Generating Regex FSMs

Visualizing a regular expressions helps you understand how they work and how they can be simplified. Until you master the regex execution model in your mind, you could have a notebook with you to construct a finite state machine for each regular expression you encounter. If you want to save time, you can also use some online services.

`http://ivanzuzak.info/noam/webapps/fsm_simulator/` simulates the execution of a regular expression matching a given string. It not only creates automata for you but also shows the execution of the matching algorithm character by character. Unfortunately, the language of the automaton is limited, as we can only concatenate strings, use the *or* operator, and use the Kleene (*) operator for indicating any number of occurrences. We can also use parentheses for grouping. Using the plus symbol instead of the pipe is slightly inconvenient because in this special dialect, plus means alternative execution and not the "at least once" repeat modifier. In exchange for the semantic difficulties, this software shows you three different types of simplified automata that can be used to match your strings. The constructs in this book have been very close to the *eNFA* construct.

`http://ivanzuzak.info/noam/webapps/regex_simplifier/` shows you how to simplify regular expressions. For instance, the expression containing the words *list*, *lost*, and *lust* is simplified as follows:

Input: list+lost+lust

R1    list+lost+lust

Rule (ab+ac) => a(b+c)
R2    l(ist+ost)+lust

Rule (ab+ac) => a(b+c)
R3    l((ist+ost)+ust)

Rule (ab+cb) => (a+c)b
R4    l(((**is**+os)t)+ust)

Rule (a) => a
R5    l((**is**+os)t+ust)

Rule (ab+cb) => (a+c)b
R6    l(((**is**+os)+us)t)

Rule (ab+cb) => (a+c)b
R7    l((((i+o)s)+us)t)

Rule (a) => a
R8    l(((i+o)s+us)t)

Rule (ab+cb) => (a+c)b
R9    l((((i+o)+u)s)t)

Rule ab(cd) => abcd
R10   l(((i+o)+u)s)t

```
Rule ab(cd) => abcd
R11  l((i+o)+u)st
```

```
Rule (a+(b+c)) => a+b+c
R12  l(i+o+u)st
```

`https://regexper.com/`[6] constructs an execution graph from a JavaScript regular expression. For instance, check out the representation of a complex JavaScript regular expression online.[7] If you study the graph, you can easily reverse engineer what each meta character means. If this regular expression seems intimidating for you, don't worry, because we all have trouble reading expressions like this one.

This graph representation has little to do with the finite state automata because in the regexper graph, edges do not consume characters. In this graph, nodes consume characters, and edges can be selected in a nondeterministic way. Also notice that edges may have conditions on them such as *1..3 times* or *1+ times*. The FSM representation of such edges may be completely different. This is a simplification for the sake of understandability.

`https://www.debuggex.com/`[8] uses the same format as regexper, and the interface helps you visualize how a regular expression matches a string character by character. You can use JavaScript, Python, and generic PCRE syntax.

`https://regexr.com/`[9] gives you a verbal explanation and cheat sheet for JavaScript, as well as the generic PCRE syntax.

---

[6]`https://regexper.com/#%2Flist%7Clost%7Clust%2F`
[7]`https://regexper.com/#%2F%5E(l%2Bi%3Fs*t%7B3%7D%24%7C%5BlL%5Dost%7B2%2C%7D%7C(lu)*st%7B1%2C4%7D%5Cd%5Cd%5B%5Eabc1-3%5D)%2F`
[8]`https://www.debuggex.com/`
[9]`https://regexr.com/`

`https://regex101.com/`[10] is another handy tool for testing whether a regular expression matches a string. PCRE (PHP), JavaScript, Python, and GoLang are all usable. The tool can also generate code for C#, Java, Ruby, Rust, and Perl 5.

`http://qfsm.sourceforge.net/download.html`[11] is my favorite finite state machine designer tool. You can visualize and simulate finite state machines conveniently.

# Summary

In this chapter, you learned the fundamentals of visualizing the execution of simple regular expressions with finite state machines. We concluded that the execution of state machines can be deterministic or nondeterministic, depending on the way how regular expressions are simplified.

Deterministic execution can be visualized using a deterministic finite automaton. Creating this automaton is expensive, but determining whether a regular expression matches a string is cheap in terms of execution time.

Nondeterministic execution can be visualized using a nondeterministic finite automaton. Creating this automaton is cheap, but executing whether a regular expression matches a string is expensive in terms of execution time.

As success is always cheaper than a failure during runtime, we tend to favor nondeterministic execution to avoid losing too much time with optimization.

We concluded this chapter with some simple considerations for optimizing regular expressions and some tools that visualize, test, simplify, or debug regular expressions.

So far, you have used a limited subset of regular expressions. In the next chapter, you will extend this subset with repeat modifiers.

---

[10]`https://regex101.com/`
[11]`http://qfsm.sourceforge.net/download.html`

# CHAPTER 5

# Repeat Modifiers

In Chapter 1, I explained that regular expressions are imperative. Imperative languages come with control structures. When developing software using a programming language, we use the following control structures:

- *Branching*: In most programming languages, we use if statements and switches. In regular expressions, we branch off using the | metasyntax character or using character sets. An | structure vaguely corresponds to an if-else structure, and a character set vaguely corresponds to a switch statement. An example of character sets is [ab]. Read it like a|b. In other words, choose either a or b.

- *Loops*: In most programming languages, we use loops such as the for loop or the while loop. *Repeat modifiers* are similar structures to loops in regular expressions.

© Zsolt Nagy 2018
Z. Nagy, *Regex Quick Syntax Reference*, https://doi.org/10.1007/978-1-4842-3876-9_5

Table 5-1 describes the repeat modifiers that are available to use.

***Table 5-1.*** *Repeat Modifiers*

| Repeat Modifier (PCRE) | Description |
| --- | --- |
| + | Match at least once |
| ? | Match at most once |
| * | Match any number of times |
| {min,max} | Match at least min times, and at most max times |
| {n} | Match exactly n times |

Table 5-1 shows the PCRE syntax only. There are some differences in other dialects. We will tackle those differences in the description of each repeat modifier.

# Backtracking

When performing a match, we can match a character, a set, or a sequence of characters. Here are some examples:

- ab+ matches an a and then at least one b. Matching strings are ab, abb, abbb, and so on.

- [ab]+ matches any number of a or b character in any order, assuming the matched sequence is at least one character long. Matching strings are a, b, aa, ab, ba, bb, aaa, aab, and so on.

- (ab)+ matches at least one ab sequence. Matching strings are ab, abab, ababab, and so on.

In most programming languages, we use loops for iteration. We
normally execute a loop a fixed number of times, moving forward in
execution. This is where regular expressions differ from other languages.
Regex repeat modifiers may unloop themselves. The process of unlooping
is called *backtracking*.

Backtracking may occur whenever we have a degree of
nondeterminism in our regular expression. Nondeterminism is brought by
alternative execution and repeat modifiers. It is easy to see that selection
and iteration are similar in nature. For instance, the repeat modifier a+ is
nothing other than an infinite sequence.

a|aa|aaa|aaaa|aaaaa|...

For instance, in JavaScript, suppose we are matching the aa string
against the regular expression /^[ab]+a$/.

```
> /^[ab]+a$/.test( 'aa' )
true
```

This matching returns true, but the execution becomes interesting, as
shown in Figure 5-1.

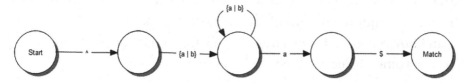

***Figure 5-1.*** *Backtracking in nondeterministic FSMs*

Notice that the ^ and $ state transitions do not read any characters
from the string, but they fix the position from which a string is parsed. The
fixed start and end anchors guard the match state such that the whole
string has to be parsed.

Suppose you have a token, and you move it among the states of the automaton to match the previous regular expression.

From the start state, the ^ anchor lets us pass at the start of the string to the first intermediate state. We then consume an a character to move to the middle state. Suppose we are using the loop with label {a|b} to consume the second a character and stay in the same state. After consuming the second a character, our string ends, and we are not in a match state.

Therefore, we have to backtrack, unlooping the [ab]+ repeat modifier once. Then we consume the second a character via the other arrow, moving us to the last intermediate state in the automaton. As the only arrow moving out from this state is the $, we have to check whether we have reached the end of the string. Yes, we have, so we successfully reach the match state.

Let's examine each repeat modifier in more depth.

# Match at Least Once

In BRE, we have to use the * to represent the + repeat modifier. a+ becomes aa*. In other words, matching an a character and at least zero more a characters is equivalent to matching at least one a character.

In EMACS and VIM, you have to escape the + operator. a+ becomes a\+. In all other dialects, we use the following:

- a+ to denote matching the a character at least once

- [ab]+ to denote matching the a or the b character at least once

- (ab)+ to denote matching the ab sequence at least once

The finite state machine belonging to a+ is as shown in Figure 5-2.

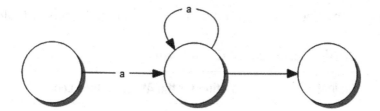

**Figure 5-2.**  /a+/

We first match an a character, and then we match any number of a characters. The next loop may be an empty transition, or we may simplify the automaton by matching the next character.

For instance, we can construct two different automata for the regular expression /a+b/, as shown in Figure 5-3 and Figure 5-4.

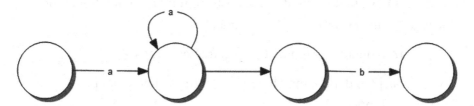

**Figure 5-3.**  /a+b/ with empty arrow

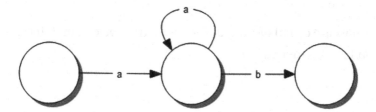

**Figure 5-4.**  /a+b/ without empty arrow

The two automata are equivalent, assuming that we can freely move forward along the empty arrow, without reading any characters.

Let's summarize the *at least once* loop for different dialects in Table 5-2.

***Table 5-2.*** *At Least Once Loop*

| Dialect | Notation for the At Least Once Loop |
|---|---|
| BRE | None; use aa* |
| ERE, PCRE, Perl 6 | a+ |
| EMACS, VIM | a\+ |

# Match at Most Once: Optionals

Optionals are not supported in BRE. Optionals have to be escaped in EMACS and VIM. In the rest of the dialects, optionals are written in the same way as the *at least once* meta character:

- a? to denote matching the a character at most once

- [ab]? to denote matching the a or the b character at most once

- (ab)? to denote matching the ab sequence at most once

Optionals are called optionals because either we can match them once or we don't match them at all.

The finite state machine belonging to an optional matching a? is shown in Figure 5-5.

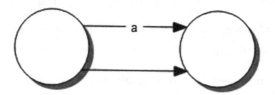

***Figure 5-5.*** */a?/*

Notice the empty arrow. When taking the bottom path, no characters are consumed from the string we attempt to match.

# Match Any Number of Times

This operator is available in all dialects without escaping. The expression a* looks the same in all dialects and matches a sequence of a characters of any lengths, including the empty string. The finite state automaton form of the match is straightforward, as shown in Figure 5-6.

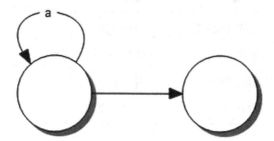

***Figure 5-6.*** */a*/*

Parentheses and brackets can be used in the same way as the + and the operators.

- a* denotes matching any number of a characters.

- [ab]* denotes matching the a or b character any number of times.

- (ab)* denotes matching the ab sequence any number of times.

Don't forget to escape the parentheses with \( and \) in EMACS and VIM.

# Fixed-Range Matching

Suppose we want to match the a character at least twice and at most 5 times. Different dialects support this in different ways, as shown in Table 5-3.

*Table 5-3. Matching the character a at least twice, and at most 5 times*

| Dialect | Notation |
| --- | --- |
| BRE, EMACS | /a\{2,5\}/ |
| VIM | /a\{2,5}/ |
| ERE, PCRE | /a{2,5}/ |
| Perl 6 | / a ** 2..5 / |

In most programming languages, we use the PCRE dialect: /a{2,5}/. Focus on your own use cases.

The finite state machine form looks verbose because we have to expand every option. Matching two to five times means we have to construct a route for matching twice, three times, four times, and five times, as shown in Figure 5-7.

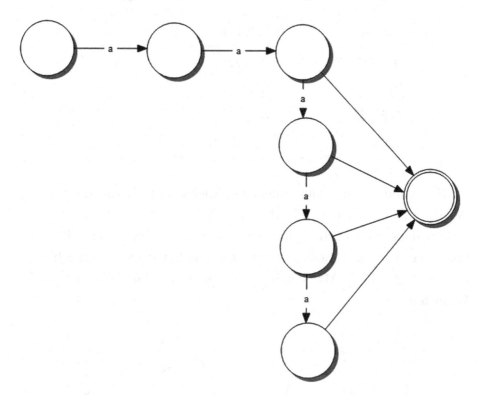

**Figure 5-7.**  /a{2,5}/

In practice, most regex engines represent this repeat modifier as an *(asterisk). An asterisk is interpreted as *any number of times* match and use internal counters to meet the required conditions.

Note that it is possible to leave out the maximum value of the range. To match at least two a characters, you have to use the notation shown in Table 5-4.

**Table 5-4.** *Matching at least two a characters*

| Dialect | Notation |
|---|---|
| BRE, EMACS | /a\{2,\}/ |
| VIM | /a\{2,}/ |
| ERE, PCRE | /a{2,}/ |
| Perl 6 | / a ** 2..* / |

Notice the maximum amount is simply left out in all dialects except Perl 6, where an * denotes the arbitrary value.

The finite state machine form of /a{2,}/ is a lot less complex than the FSM belonging to the bounded repeat modifier. In fact, this machine is equivalent to the FSM belonging to the expression /aaa*/, as shown in Figure 5-8.

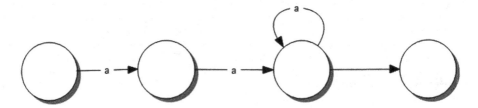

*Figure 5-8. /a{2,}/*

In theory, the upper limit is unbounded. In practice, this upper limit depends on the implementation of the regex virtual machine. The upper limit restriction may be a low value like 256. In other languages, this value is 32767, which is one less than the maximum value of a 2-byte-long unsigned integer. Be careful when using regular expressions with big upper limits.

Also note, in some languages like Python, the real maximum limit is infinity, but you may easily get an overflow error if this limit is too big.

# Loop Exactly *n* Times

Let's examine the shorthand for the expression /aa/ in all dialects, as shown in Table 5-5.

*Table 5-5.* *Shorthand for /aa/*

| Dialect | Notation |
|---|---|
| BRE, EMACS | /a\{2\}/ |
| VIM | /a\{2}/ |
| ERE, PCRE | /a{2}/ |
| Perl 6 | / a ** 2 / |

This means we loop through the a character exactly twice. When there is a complex expression instead of a or the number of repetitions is a lot more than 2, the shorthand actually becomes shorter than the original version of /aa/.

The finite state machine belonging to this loop is straightforward, as shown in Figure 5-9.

*Figure 5-9.* /aa/

As you can see, the state machine matches the FSM of /aa/.

# Greedy Repeat Modifiers

You have already seen the meta characters for greedy repeat modifiers in Table 5-1.

All these repeat modifiers are *greedy* by default. This means the repeat modifiers consume as many characters from the matched string as possible and backtrack character by character.

As an extreme example, suppose we are matching the string 'The lost list' using the regular expression /^.*list$/.

As the * repeat modifier is greedy, .* consumes the whole string first, just to conclude that we are at the end of the string and we have yet to match the character l. In case of a failure, we backtrack.

Repeat modifiers consume characters in a greedy way, and they backtrack as little as possible. Therefore, we backtrack just one character. After the backtracking, .* matches The lost lis, and the next character to be consumed is t. As t is not equal to l, we backtrack.

Now .* becomes The lost li, and we are trying to match s against l. This doesn't work, so we backtrack.

Now .* becomes The lost l, and we are trying to match i against l. This doesn't work, so we backtrack.

Now .* becomes The lost , and we are trying to match l against l. This succeeds, so we continue matching the rest of the string with the rest of the regex pattern. As we succeed matching the whole string and we reach the end, we exit the regex matching with success.

In this example, we just backtracked four times. But imagine if we had megabytes of text; one .* construct may read the whole file before evaluating the rest of the regular expression. Therefore, proceed with .*- like constructs with caution. There is almost always a more optimal way to describe a pattern.

Backtracking is introduced because our state machine is nondeterministic. In /^.*list$/, in each step, as long as we are in the .* loop and an l character is coming, we have to decide whether we are matching a . character or we are matching an l. This is the nondeterminism that causes backtracking.

One way to combat backtracking is to make the nondeterministic state machine deterministic. This may require an exponential number of steps with respect to the size of the input. Only a few regex virtual machines do this because the effort rarely pays off.

Another solution is to use loops that match and backtrack according to a different strategy.

# Lazy Repeat Modifiers

You have seen that greed sometimes leads to bad performance. What you have not seen is the relationship between greed and correctness. Greed can sometimes lead to incorrect results.

For instance, suppose you want to create a global regular expression in JavaScript that matches *all* questions in a Spanish text. In Spanish, the syntax of a question is as follows:

¿<SENTENCE>?

Assuming there are no newline characters, it makes sense to match a sentence using the following regular expression:

```
let regex = /¿.+\?/g
```

Let's test our regex on some questions.

```
let text = '¿Tienes animals en casa? ¿Dónde está la biblioteca?';

> text.match( regex );
["¿Tienes animals en casa? ¿Dónde está la biblioteca?"]
```

Oops, something seems to be wrong. Both questions were returned as one result. Why?

Because our .+ repeat modifier is greedy, that's why! .+ doesn't care that a \? character is coming. We read the question mark as an arbitrary character.

This is why repeat modifiers have a *lazy* version of repeat modifiers in most dialects.

Lazy repeat modifiers match the *minimum* number of characters that are absolutely necessary by executing the body of the repeat modifier as few times as possible. Once the expression fails and we have to backtrack, we now add characters instead of removing them.

The syntax of lazy repeat modifiers is as follows: in EMACS, PCRE, and Perl 6, we simply add a question mark (?) after the repeat modifier.

- a*? matches zero or more a characters and attempts to match as few a characters as possible.

- a+? matches one or more a characters and attempts to match as few a characters as possible.

- a?? matches zero or one a characters, first attempting not to match the a character.

- a{1,2}? attempts to match the a character once or twice, first trying to match it once. In Perl 6, the equivalent syntax is a **? 1..2.

Let's see our JavaScript example:

```
let regex = /¿.+?\?/g
let text = '¿Tienes animals en casa? ¿Dónde está la
biblioteca?';

text.match( regex );
```

The return value matches the two sentences properly.

(2) ["¿Tienes animals en casa?", "¿Dónde está la biblioteca?"]

Note that regardless if you want to use greedy or lazy repeat modifiers, it makes sense to restrict the search space. We can exclude the first character following the repeat modifier from the possible first characters inside the repeated sequence. This means we are better off excluding the \? character from the arbitrary . character class. We can perform the exclusion by defining the [^\?] character set. Read it as "an arbitrary character except the question mark."

```
regex = /¿[^\?]+\?/g;
```

```
> text.match( regex )
(2) ["¿Tienes animals en casa?", "¿Dónde está la biblioteca?"]
```

---

**Tip**    Always attempt to make the first character of the sequence inside the repeat modifier body and the first character after the repeat modifier mutually exclusive to avoid nondeterministic branching and backtracking.

---

Now we have the two sentences one by one, as two separate matches of the global regular expression. To get some more practice with lazy repeat modifiers, let's match /^.*?list$/ against the text The lost list.

- The is matched by .*, before we attempt to match list$ on lost list. We do consume l from the string, but then, the letter o does not match i from the pattern, so we backtrack.

- The lost is matched by .*. We now attempt to match the list$ pattern with list. We succeed. No more backtracking is needed.

In this example, the result was the same, but the number of backtracking operations was lower.

You may ask the question, when it is worth using a lazy repeat modifier, and when it is worth using a greedy repeat modifier? The answer is not obvious.

- You may want to use one version or another for correctness reasons. See the Spanish questions, for example. Whenever you have to match a pattern where there is a starting sign and an ending sign and the expressions may not be nested, a minimal loop is correct.

- When correctness does not matter, you can sometimes intuitively figure out which pattern to use. Remember, a match is always cheaper than failure; therefore, it is worth optimizing for faster matching.

# Possessive Repeat Modifiers

A possessive repeat modifier executes as a greedy repeat modifier does with one exception: once a possessive structure backtracks, it fails. Instead of backtracking just one iteration, the possessive repeat modifier just fully gives up, reverting all iterations. Either we greedily match as many iterations of the possessive loop as possible or we don't match any iterations at all.

Possessive repeat modifiers are available in PCRE and in Perl 6.

In most PCRE languages, we write a + after the symbol of the corresponding greedy repeat modifier to indicate that it is possessive, yielding a*+, a++, a?+, a{1,2}+ loops.

In Perl 6, we write a : after the repeat modifier: a*:, a+:, a?:, a **: 1..2.

Some languages like JavaScript don't have possessive repeat modifiers. It is still possible to emulate them with a construct we are not yet familiar with. Write down this expression: (?=(a+))\1. Once you know what a positive lookahead is and how capture groups work, you can verify that the expression (?=(a+))\1 is equivalent to a++, assuming that there are no other open parentheses in front of this expression. The equivalence is not fully strict, though, because a capture group is introduced to construct the possessive repeat modifier. The introduced capture group may offset the numbering of other capture groups behind this capture group.

*I encourage you to play around with possessive repeat modifiers in regex101.com.[1] You can see the matching executed in a step-by-step fashion if you use the regex debugger belonging to the PHP (PCRE) syntax.*

For instance, the expression /a++b/ matches any string containing the sequence ab. The pattern a++ matches the a character, and then b is matched.

The expression /a++a/ never matches any strings. This is because a++ is possessive, so it eats up all the a characters before attempting to match another a character. As this a character is never found, the regex engine backtracks fully and fails. Unlike /a+a/, we cannot backtrack just one character in /a++a/. Therefore, no strings will ever match the regex /a++a/.

As a rule of thumb, we can conclude that the first character of the sequence we are trying to match in a possessive repeat modifier may never follow the repeat modifier itself. Otherwise, we will never get a match.

---

[1] www.regex101.com

# Summary

Most programming languages implement *sequence, selection*, and *iteration*. While sequence and selection are obvious in regular expressions, there are many ways to perform iteration. You have learned five basic ways to iterate a pattern. The + symbol indicates matching a character or a sequence at least once. The ? symbol matches at most once, and the * symbol matches any number of times. We can also formulate cardinality restrictions by specifying the minimum and the maximum of allowed occurrence count. We can also repeat a sequence exactly a specified number of times.

You also used the notation [ab] to select either the a character *or* the b character. I will expand on this concept in the next chapter by introducing *character sets*.

Generic repeat modifiers are greedy: they attempt to match a maximal number of characters. Backtracking is minimal; you remove one character from the matched string during each backtracking attempt.

You can add a ? at the end of the repeat modifier to get a lazy repeat modifier, which does minimal matching and increases the number of matched characters one by one after each backtracking.

You can add a + at the end of the repeat modifier to get a possessive repeat modifier, which does maximal matching and fails during any backtracking attempt.

# CHAPTER 6

# Character Sets and Character Classes

The previous chapter introduced finite state machines to make regular expressions easier to understand. In this chapter, you will learn the tools you need to create more complex finite state machines to perform advanced pattern matching tasks with regular expressions.

We will build on Chapter 2, assuming that you know how to handle literal characters, concatenation, the *or* operator, the dot character, grouping operators with parentheses, anchored start and end, and modifiers.

## Character Sets

A character set matches strings containing any of the characters in the set.

In Perl 6, character sets are enumerated inside <[ and ]>.

In all other dialects, including all other programming languages and text editors, we use brackets: [ and ].

© Zsolt Nagy 2018
Z. Nagy, *Regex Quick Syntax Reference*, https://doi.org/10.1007/978-1-4842-3876-9_6

The character set for a string containing at least one binary digit is as follows:

- /<[01]>/ in Perl 6

- /[01]/ in all other dialects

The expression [01] matches a 0 *or* a 1 character.

As I have already introduced the *or* operator, it is easy to conclude that the previous character set is equivalent to the following:

- /0\|1/ in EMACS and VIM

- /0|1/ in ERE, Perl 6, and PCRE (including all programming languages)

Regex engines tend to build an internal representation of sets using bitmasks. Therefore, checking character sets is often just as efficient as matching single characters.

In the finite state machine representation, there is only one edge connecting two states, as shown in Figure 6-1.

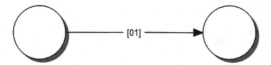

***Figure 6-1.*** */[01]/*

I used the [01] character set notation to indicate the bitmask.

# Character Set Ranges

Imagine that your next task is to represent an octal digit and a hexadecimal digit. In PCRE, knowing what you already know, you could use the following syntax:

- /[01234567]/ for an octal digit

- /[0123456789abcdefABCDEF]/ for a hexadecimal
  digit

Regular expressions allow you to define ranges using the - character in most dialects. Only Perl 6 is different, where you have to use the .. character.[1]

Therefore, the octal digit becomes as follows:

- /<[0..7]>/ in Perl 6

- /[0-7]/ in all other dialects

The range 0-7 is equivalent to 01234567.

The task of writing a hexadecimal digit seems to be a bit more complicated at first glance. Writing /[0-9]|[a-f]|[A-F]/ is completely valid, but the syntax looks too complicated.

Recalling the equivalence of ranges and their enumerations, we can conclude the following:

- 0123456789 is equivalent to 0-9.

- abcdef is equivalent to a-f.

- ABCDEF is equivalent to A-F.

---

[1]In Perl 6, the - character denotes subtraction between character sets and negation of character sets.

As a consequence, `0123456789abcdefABCDEF` is equivalent to `0-9a-fA-F`. Therefore, the hexadecimal digit becomes the following:

- `/<[0..9a..fA..F]>/` in Perl 6

- `/[0-9a-fA-F]/` in all other dialects

# Exclusions from Character Sets

You saw that character sets are represented by bitmasks in most regex interpreters. You will now figure out how to invert these bits.

In Perl 6, placing a - in front of the opening bracket inverts the character set. This minus meta character can also be used in front of character set classes. See the next section for more details on character classes.

In all other dialects, the inverter character is the ^ operator, placed inside the brackets in front of the character enumeration, range, or class.

For instance, characters that are not hexadecimal digits are defined as follows:

- `/<-[0..9a..fA..F]>/` in Perl 6

- `/[^0-9a-fA-F]/` in all other dialects

# Character Set Classes

The good news is that regex dialects allow us to specify character set classes such as digits, whitespaces, or alphanumerical characters. The bad news is each dialect does it differently.

For instance, the PHP documentation enumerates the character classes available in PHP.[2]

---

[2]`http://php.net/manual/en/regexp.reference.character-classes.php`

This simplifies the hexadecimal character example originating from character set ranges to /[[:xdigit:]]/. Notice the double brackets. The outer bracket denotes that we define a character set. The inner bracket belongs to the named character class syntax.

As a rule of thumb, always used named character classes instead of ranges and enumerations because named classes make it easier to read and maintain your expressions in the future.

**Exercise 1**: Write PHP code matching the 'Aa5h' string against the /[[:xdigit:]]/ character set class expression. Use the output generated by https://regex101.com[3] to determine the results. You can run your code online using the service www.writephponline.com/.[4]

**Solution:**

```php
$re = '/[[:xdigit:]]/';
$str = 'Aa5h';

preg_match_all($re, $str, $matches, PREG_SET_ORDER, 0);

// Print the entire match result
var_dump($matches);
```

After execution, we get the following response:

```
array(3) {
    [0]=> array(1) { [0]=> string(1) "A" }
    [1]=> array(1) { [0]=> string(1) "a" }
    [2]=> array(1) { [0]=> string(1) "5" }
}
```

This means the regular expression successfully matches the uppercase and lowercase alphabetical digits as well as the numerical digit. As h is not a hexadecimal digit, no match is returned.

---

[3]https://regex101.com
[4]www.writephponline.com/

**Exercise 2**: Write a regular expression in Perl 6 checking whether a string contains a hexadecimal character, where the alphabetical digits may be written only in uppercase. Use the Perl 6 documentation[5] to research how regular expressions are written in Perl 6, and use the service tio.run[6] to execute your code.

**Solution:**

According to the documentation, the code looks like the following:

```
if 'XXaAXX' ~~ m/<+xdigit -lower>/ {
    say "Matching character: " ~ $/;
    say "String before the match is: " ~ $/.prematch;
    say "String after the match is: " ~ $/.postmatch;
    say "Match start index: " ~ $/.from;
    say "Match end index: " ~ $/.to;
}
```

We will use the test string `'xxaAXX'` and expect that our regular expression will match only the uppercase A character at index 3, not the lowercase a character at index 2.

The regular expression /<+xdigit -lower>/ defines a character set including all hexadecimal characters and excluding lowercase letters. I could have used the abbreviation :Ll for denoting the lower class. This would have changed the regular expression to /+xdigit -:Ll/.

The syntax of the condition is equivalent to the one in the documentation, except for the more verbose messages. After executing the code using tio.run, we get the following output:

```
Matching character: A
String before the match is: XXa
String after the match is: XX
Match start index: 3
Match end index: 4
```

---

[5]https://docs.perl6.org/language/regexes
[6]https://tio.run/#perl6

Each programming language comes with its own documentation for its character classes. We have seen in the case of Perl 6 that some languages have a redundant notation, specifically, a more semantic one (`lower`) and a shorter one (`Ll`).

In JavaScript, character classes are escape sequences. See the documentation on `developer.mozilla.org`[7] for more details.

**Exercise 3**: Formulate the Perl 6 regular expression `/<+xdigit -lower>/` in JavaScript.

**Solution:**

JavaScript does not have a hexadecimal digit class. Therefore, we will simply use the decimal digit class `\d` and the range `A-F`.

The resulting regular expression is `/[\dA-F]/`.

Always look up the documentation for the exact class names, as they differ in each language. Some rules of thumb still apply, such as the following:

> `\d` stands for a digit (`[0-9]`).

> `\D` stands for a nondigit character (`[^0-9]`).

> `\s` stands for whitespace (`\s-` in EMACS; `[\t\r\n\f]`).

> `\S` stands for a nonwhitespace (`\S-` in EMACS; `[^\t\r\n\f]`).

> `\w` stands for a character typically used in identifiers (`[0-9a-zA-Z_]`).

> `\W` stands for a nonidentifier character.

[7]https://developer.mozilla.org/en-US/docs/Web/JavaScript/Reference/ Global_Objects/RegExp

# Concatenating Advanced Language Constructs

We have already covered some basic use cases for concatenating regular expression characters. For instance, the expression /re/ means we have to match the character r, followed by the character e.

Concatenation works with any regex subexpressions. Therefore, the expression

```
/\d.[^a-z][^a-z]/
```

is valid in PCRE. It matches four characters, a digit, an arbitrary character, and two characters that are not lowercase letters.

Special characters require special care. Suppose we would like to search for the expression [(1+2)*3]^2. If we fire up our JavaScript Chrome Developer Tools and execute a matching string '/[(1+2)*3]^2/' against the regex /[(1+2)*3]^2/, we are destined to fail.

```
> '[(1+2)*3]^2'.match( /[(1+2)*3]^2/ )
null
```

The reason is that we have to escape all special characters.

```
'[(1+2)*3]^2'.match( /\[\(1\+2\)\*3\]\^2/ )
["[(1+2)*3]^2", index: 0, input: "[(1+2)*3]^2"]
```

Correct me if I am wrong, but escaping seems anything but readable. Some languages such as Perl and PHP provide the \Q and \E special characters to write any characters unescaped. Whatever is written in between \Q and \E will be matched in sequence, character by character.

For instance, the PHP implementation looks like this:

```
$re = '/\Q[(1+2)*3]^2\E/';
$str = '[(1+2)*3]^2';

preg_match_all($re, $str, $matches, PREG_SET_ORDER, 0);
```

```
// Print the entire match result
var_dump($matches);
```

The output is as follows:

**array**(1) { [0]=> **array**(1) { [0]=> string(11) "[(1+2)*3]^2" } }

As this feature does not exist in JavaScript, we have the following options:

- Use an extended library such as xregexp.[8]

- Use an escaping function[9] that does the dirty work automatically.

Here's an example (which you can find online[10]):

```
RegExp.escape = function(text) {
    return text.replace(/[-[\]{}()*+?.,\\^$|#\s]/g, "\\$&");
}
```

# Summary

In this chapter, you learned to use some more advanced elements of the regular expression syntax.

- Character sets

- Character set ranges

- Exclusions from character sets

- Character set classes

I concluded this chapter with some examples concatenating regex substrings formed using the language constructs you already know.

---

[8]http://xregexp.com/

[9]https://simonwillison.net/2006/Jan/20/escape/

[10]https://stackoverflow.com/questions/6318710/
  javascript-equivalent-of-perls-q-e-or-quotemeta

# CHAPTER 7

# Substring Extraction from Regular Expressions

You read about many different use cases of regular expressions in Chapter 1. Let me repeat some of these use cases:

- – To test whether a string matches a search expression
- – To find some characters in a string
- – To replace substrings in a string matching a regex
- – To process and format user input
- – To extract information from server logs, configuration files, and text files
- – To validate input in web applications and in the terminal

Many of the use cases require that we find a *substring* of a string and extract it, reorder it, remove it, or replace it.

Regular expressions provide us with some help to perform these tasks in the form of substring extraction.

© Zsolt Nagy 2018
Z. Nagy, *Regex Quick Syntax Reference*, https://doi.org/10.1007/978-1-4842-3876-9_7

When I introduced literal characters and meta characters, I said that parentheses had two semantics: grouping characters and extracting substrings. Even in the section on regex operator precedence and parentheses in Chapter 2, I mentioned that we would use parentheses for substring extraction. Let's learn this important use case.

# Defining Capture Groups

When the regular expression substring x is in parentheses, as in (x), it is a *capture group*. Capture groups cannot be defined inside character classes.

The value of capture groups is captured and can be retrieved either inside the regular expression or using the API of the programming language you are using. Retrieval is possible only whenever the closing parenthesis in the regular expression matching process has been reached.

In all languages except Perl 6, the identifier of a capture group is a positive integer determined by the position of the opening parenthesis in the expression.

**Exercise 1**: Let's determine the capture groups in the following PCRE regular expression:

/^a(b|c(d|(e))(f))$/

**Solution:**

Table 7-1 shows the solution.

***Table 7-1.***  *Solution for Exercise 1*

| Capture Group Number | Substring Pattern |
| --- | --- |
| 1 | b\|c(d\|(e))(f) |
| 2 | d\|(e) |
| 3 | e |
| 4 | f |

The capture group number is determined by the position of the opening parenthesis.

```
/^a(b|c(d|(e))(f))$/
   ^    ^  ^    ^
   |    |  |    |
   1    2  3    4
```

# Perl 6 Capture Groups

In Perl 6, capture group numbering is different. Capture group numbering starts with zero. The capture group identifier increases in a nested hierarchical way.

On the top level, there is one capture group with the identifier 0.

```
/^a(b|c(d|(e))(f))$/
   ^
   |
   0
```

Inside capture group 0, there are two capture groups on the next level: 0.0 and 0.1. The capture group numbering starts like this:

```
/^a(b|c(d|(e))(f))$/
     ^        ^
     |        |
    0.0      0.1
```

Inside the capture group 0.0, there is one more capture group.

```
/^a(b|c(d|(e))(f))$/
        ^
        |
      0.0.0
```

***Table 7-2.*** *Perl 6 capture group numbering*

| Perl 6 Capture Group Number | Substring Pattern |
| --- | --- |
| 0 | b\|c(d\|(e))(f) |
| 0.0 | d\|(e) |
| 0.0.0 | e |
| 0.1 | f |

# Retrieval of Captured Substrings

Check out the documentation of the programming language you are using. As an example, we will retrieve substrings in the following languages:

- JavaScript

- PHP

- Python

- Perl 5

We will use the same example as earlier. Suppose we want to retrieve the currency, the numeric price value, and the full price with currency in a string in this format:

```
Price: €19.00
```

The regular expression matching this string is as follows:

```
/^Price: [€\$]\d\d\.\d\d$/
```

We have to escape the dollar sign as a currency because $ is a meta character denoting an end-of-string or end-of-line anchor. We also have to escape a dot because it is a meta character denoting one arbitrary character.

Let's add some parentheses for the substrings we have to capture.

```
/^Price: (([€\$])(\d\d\.\d\d))$/
```

The added capture groups contain the data shown in Table 7-3.

*Table 7-3. Data for Capture Groups*

| Capture Group Number | Data |
| --- | --- |
| 1 | Full price |
| 2 | Currency symbol |
| 3 | Numeric price |

Let's explore the retrieval of the three capture groups.

99

# JavaScript

The API works as follows:

- `regex.exec( str )`

- `str.match( regex )`

These return all the capture groups defined in regex when matching str.

```javascript
const regex = /^Price: (([€\$])(\d\d\.\d\d))$/;
const str = 'Price: €19.00';

const matches = regex.exec( str );
// str.match( regex ); // does the same

console.table( matches );
```

```
(index) Value
0        "Price: €19.00"
1        "€19.00"
2        "€"
3        "19.00"
index    0
input    "Price: €19.00"
```

As a side note, if you don't yet know `console.table`, check out my article on the console API.[1]

---

[1]www.zsoltnagy.eu/understanding-the-console-api-in-javascript-7-tips-
for-smoother-debugging/

# PHP

We will use preg_match_all( $regex, $str, $result ). PHP returns all the capture groups inside the $result array.

```
$regex = "/^Price: ((€|\$)(\d\d\.\d\d))$/";
$str = "Price: €19.00";

preg_match_all($regex, $str, $result);
print_r($result);
```

Execute the code, for example, in the PHP Sandbox.[2] The result is as follows:

```
Array
(
    [0] => Array
        (
            [0] => Price: €19.00
        )
    [1] => Array
        (
            [0] => €19.00
        )
    [2] => Array
        (
            [0] => €
        )
    [3] => Array
        (
            [0] => 19.00
        )
)
```

---

[2]http://sandbox.onlinephpfunctions.com/

# Python

Let's recall the code we saw when we first tested regular expressions with Python, and let's place the correct regex and test_str values in there.

```python
import re

regex = r"^Price: ((€|\$)(\d\d\.\d\d))$"

test_str = "Price: €19.00"

matches = re.finditer(regex, test_str)

for matchNum, match in enumerate(matches):
    matchNum = matchNum + 1

    print ("Match {matchNum} was found at {start}-{end}: {match}"
        .format(
            matchNum = matchNum,
            start = match.start(),
            end = match.end(),
            match = match.group()
        )
    )

    for groupNum in range(0, len(match.groups())):
        groupNum = groupNum + 1

        print ("Group {groupNum} found at {start}-{end}: {group}"
            .format(
                groupNum = groupNum,
                start = match.start(groupNum),
                end = match.end(groupNum),
                group = match.group(groupNum)
            )
        )
```

Once we paste this code in the Python shell,[3] the result becomes visible.

```
Match 1 was found at 0-13: Price: €19.00
Group 1 found at 7-13: €19.00
Group 2 found at 7-8: €
Group 3 found at 8-13: 19.00
```

As you can see, the capture groups are accessible via the match object.

Yes, this was the promised foreshadowing from the first introduction of the same Python code. Originally, the same code didn't find any capture groups in the expression, but now you can see that the inner for loop prints out the capture groups one by one.

# Perl 5

We have seen that a simple match can be executed using the =~operator.

```
if ( "Price: €19.00" =~ /^Price: ((€|\$)(\d\d\.\d\d))$/ ) {
    print "Match";
}
```

We have already seen a few variables that provide us with some context to the match, such as the following:

```
if ( "Price: €19.00" =~ /^Price: ((€|\$)(\d\d\.\d\d))$/ ) {
    print "String before the match: ", $`, "\n";
    print "String after the match:", $', "\n";
    print "Matched string:", $&, "\n";
}
```

Similarly, there are variables defined for each capture group in the form of $1, $2, $3, and so on.

---

[3]https://www.python.org/shell/

```
if ( "Price: €19.00" =~ /^Price: ((€|\$)(\d\d\.\d\d))$/ ) {
    print "String before the match: ", $`, "\n";
    print "String after the match:", $', "\n";
    print "Matched string:", $&, "\n";
    print "First capture group:", $1, "\n";
    print "Second capture group:", $2, "\n";
    print "Third capture group:", $3, "\n";
}
```

The result of the execution is as follows:

```
String before the match:
String after the match:
Matched string:Price: €19.00
First capture group: €19.00
Second capture group: €
Third capture group:19.00
```

# Reusing Captured Substrings Within a Regex

Suppose we are interested in extracting a price in between any positive number of highlighter characters. The following strings should all be matches:

```
****€19.00****
*-*€19.00*-*
--€19.00--
```

The following inputs are invalid:

```
€19.00     // no highlighter
*€19.00**  // length before and after don't match
**€19.00-- // character sequences don't match
++€19.00++ // not accepted characters
```

Let's start with the assembly of the regular expression assuming that the price ranges between 1.00 and 9999.99 euros, as shown in Table 7-4.

*Table 7-4. Assembling a regular expression matching a price label*

| Constructed Regex | Explanation |
|---|---|
| /^$/ | We are matching for the whole string, not just substrings. |
| /^[\*-]+$/ | We start with any number of highlighter characters. |
| /^[\*-]+€\.$/ | We place the euro sign and the escaped dot character in the expression. |
| /^[\*-]+€\d{1,4}\.\d{2}$/ | Then we add the digits, making sure that there are always two digits after the decimal point. |

We are now stuck. Continuing with the assembly of the regular expression is not possible with the constructs you have learned so far.

This is where we need to know what was exactly matched before the euro sign. This is when reusing a previously captured substring becomes useful, as shown in Table 7-5.

*Table 7-5. Using a backreference to match a price label*

| Constructed Regex | Explanation |
|---|---|
| /^([\*-]+)€\d{1,4}\.\d{2}$/ | Capture the substring that has to be repeated |
| /^([\*-]+)€\d{1,4}\.\d{2}\1$/ | Access and insert the exact substring matched in capture group 1 using \1 |

Let's test our regular expression in JavaScript using the Chrome Developer Tools console.

```
/^([\*-]+)€\d{1,4}\.\d{2}\1$/.exec( '****€19.00****' )
> {
    0: "****€19.00****",
    1: "****",
    index: 0,
    input: "****€19.00****"
  }
```

\1 is called a *backreference*. A backreference rematches the same characters already matched in a character group.

**Example**: Create a PCRE-compatible regular expression that detects four-letter palindrome[4] words.

**Solution:**

We need to use the usual start and end anchors, followed by two arbitrary characters. As we need to capture these characters, we put them in parentheses. Then we need to swap these characters by including them backward, using the backreferences \2 and \1.

```
/^(.)(.)\2\1$/
```

In Perl 6, backreferences are variables defined by writing a $ sign in front of the capture group number. Here's an example: $0.

Always test your backreferences. Whenever they don't exist, the erroneous behavior differs from environment to environment.

# Capture Groups and Performance

Unfortunately, the semantics of parentheses are overloaded. This can be dangerous when it comes to performance.

---

[4]https://en.wikipedia.org/wiki/Palindrome

When we learn the basics of regular expressions, we learn the natural semantics of parentheses, which is to override the precedence of operators. However, be aware of the following:

---

Every set of parentheses creates a capture group, regardless of whether we need them. As capture groups are expensive, the performance of our regular expression is affected by adding the overhead of maintaining the capture groups to the execution time of the expression.

---

The overhead of maintaining the capture groups can be expensive. The regex engine has to add and remove characters from active capture groups while reading a character or backtracking.

To avoid the performance penalty, it is possible to define parentheses that do not create capture groups. These parentheses are only there for overriding precedence, as shown in Table 7-6.

*Table 7-6.* *Non-capturing parentheses*

| Language | No-Capture Parentheses |
| --- | --- |
| EMACS | /(?:exp)/ |
| ERE,PCRE | /(?:exp)/ |
| Perl 6 | / [exp] / |
| VIM | /\%(exp)/ |

In most programming languages and in EMACS, ?: after the start parentheses defines the group to be noncapturing. In Perl 6, the character set syntax of earlier languages is used for this purpose. This is because Perl 6 is a new language, and time has proven that we need noncapturing parentheses more often than character sets.

VIM came up with some weird notation that I find highly illogical in hindsight. Back when the notation was invented, it must have been innovative.

# Extensions to Capture Groups

Some PCRE-based languages offer even more features.

Ruby and Perl support backreferences relative to the capture group we are in. The syntax differs from implementation to implementation. An example in Ruby looks like `((.)\k<-1>)+`, where the backreference is `\k<-1>`, indicating the capture group just before the backreference.

In some languages, *forward references* make it possible to reference to a future capture group. Here's an example: `(\3\2(.)(.))*`.

One problem with capture group numbering is maintainability. Even after the extraction, the variables `$1`, `$2`, and so on, are not too semantic. Python addresses this problem by allowing a name tag in a regular expression. Here's an example: `(?P<name>value)`. In ES2018, the 2018 version of JavaScript, named capture groups also appear in the form `(?<name>value)`.

# Summary

In this chapter, you learned the basics of creating capture groups and learned the rules of capture group numbering. You also retrieved captured strings in four different languages.

As capture groups may be expensive to maintain, you looked at a way to define noncapturing parentheses to avoid the performance penalty.

# CHAPTER 8

# Lookahead and Lookbehind

Anchors such as ^, $, and the \b boundary character are zero-length assertions that filter matches based on special conditions. These conditions restrict the position of the first or last character of the match. We will now do something similar, but this time, we will restrict the position of some characters in the expression with respect to other characters in the string. *Lookahead* and *Lookbehind* are two zero-length assertions that accomplish this.

For the sake of simplicity, we will restrict this chapter to PCRE-compatible languages and Perl 6.

## Lookahead

A *lookahead* matches characters but reverts the actions upon success. There are two types of lookaheads: *positive* and *negative*.

We use a positive lookahead if our match has to be followed by a certain pattern.

We use a *negative lookahead* if our match *should not be followed by* a certain pattern. Table 8-1 shows the syntax.

***Table 8-1.*** *Syntax for Lookahead*

| Lookahead Type | PCRE Syntax | Perl 6 Syntax |
|---|---|---|
| Positive | `(?=pattern)` | `<?before pattern>` |
| Negative | `(?!pattern)` | `<!before pattern>` |
| Word boundary | `\b` | `>>` |

The syntax may not be too pleasing to the eye, especially in the case of the negative assertion. However, my experience is that you will get used to it if you use it. Until then, keep your cheat sheet with you.

Lookaheads do not capture substrings, similarly to `(?:pattern)`.

As the lookahead may contain any literal or meta character, capture groups defined inside a lookahead will capture the matched string. In fact, this is the only way to capture the value of the lookahead.

The lookahead `(?=.c)` in `/a(?=.c)b/` matches the string abc as follows:

1. First we read a.

2. Then we enter the lookahead, memorizing the index 1 pointing at character b of abc.

3. We match the character b as an arbitrary character inside the lookahead.

4. We match the character c in the lookahead.

5. As the lookahead succeeds, we exit from the lookahead construct with success and revert to position 1 in the string.

6.  We match character b in the string.

7.  The regex matching succeeds, and the substring
    "ab" starting at position 0 is returned. Word
    boundaries work like a positive lookahead.

**Example 1**: Using the PCRE dialect, match list, lost, or lust in a string such that the matched string should end a nonwhitespace character sequence.

**Solution:**

We can simply use a word boundary anchor at the end of the matched sequence.

```
/l[iou]st\b/
```

**Example 2**: Suppose the following championship classification is given in the form of a JavaScript template literal:

```
const classification = `
    1st D.Okada (5) 97Pts
    2nd J.Newtown (27) 78Pts
`;
```

Create a regular expression that matches all scores. A score is a non-negative integer in front of the text Pt.

**Solution:**

/\d+/ matches positive integers in the form of sequences of digits.

As we need all matches, we have to apply the g modifier to the expression: /\d+/g. Let's list all the numbers from the expression.

```
> let regex = /\d+/g;
> let result = null;
> while ( result = regex.exec( classification ) ) {
    console.log( result[0] );
  }
```

1

5

97

2

27

78

Let's apply a lookahead to match the scores only. The lookahead
syntax is (?=Pt).

```
> regex = /\d+(?=Pt)/g;
> while ( result = regex.exec( classification ) ) {
    console.log( result[0] );
  }
97
78
```

# Lookbehind

A *lookbehind* is the mirror image of a lookahead. It walks backward from
the regular expression and checks whether the specified pattern matches
the string *before* the lookbehind. If the lookbehind match succeeds, the
match is reverted. The syntax is shown in Table 8-2.

*Table 8-2.* *Lookbehind Syntax*

| Lookbehind Type | PCRE Syntax | Perl 6 Syntax |
| --- | --- | --- |
| Positive | (?<=pattern) | <?after pattern> |
| Negative | (?<!pattern) | <!after pattern> |
| Word boundary | \b | << |

Opposed to lookahead, lookbehind constructs are often restricted. Restrictions differ from implementation to implementation.

Most dialects only allow patterns of fixed lengths and exclude repeat modifiers, as well as character sets. This is not universally true because Java, for instance, allows fixed-range repeat modifiers.

**Example 3**: Using PCRE, match list, lost, lust inside nonwhitespace character sequences in case they start the nonwhitespace sequence.

**Solution:**

This time the word boundary anchor is placed before the l of the matched strings.

```
PCRE:    /\bl[iou]st/
```

# Summary

A *lookahead* matches characters looking forward but reverts all actions upon success.

A *lookbehind* matches characters looking backward and reverts all actions upon success.

A word boundary anchor may work as a lookahead or as a lookbehind indicating the start or end of a nonwhitespace character sequence.

# CHAPTER 9

# Maintaining Regular Expressions

There is a common fear in the industry of writing and maintaining regular expressions. This is because as an expression becomes bigger, reading it gets harder.

This reminds me of the word *Fluessigkeitsliebhaberei* in my gym. It means the act of loving fluids. In one word. Complete nonsense. German words are long. Sometimes very long.

*Rindfleischetikettierungsueberwachungsaufgabenuebertragungsgesetz* is another example.[1] Most readers are used to reading short words. Then comes a long word like this out of the blue, and we can throw all our speed-reading experience out of the window.

Software developers are used to reading code. But code normally contains a lot of whitespaces. The following PCRE expression[2] is just like a very long German word:

```
/^(?=.*[A-Z].*[A-Z])(?=.*[!@#$&*])(?=.*[0-9].*[0-9])
(?=.*[a-z].*[a-z]).{8,}$/
```

---

[1] https://en.wikipedia.org/wiki/Rinderkennzeichnungs-_und_Rindfleis chetikettierungs%C3%BCberwachungsaufgaben%C3%BCbertragungsgesetz

[2] Source: https://stackoverflow.com/questions/5142103/regex-to-validate-password-strength. I slightly modified the expression to allow passwords longer than eight characters. I also changed the minimum number of lowercase letters from three to two.

© Zsolt Nagy 2018

Z. Nagy, *Regex Quick Syntax Reference*, https://doi.org/10.1007/978-1-4842-3876-9_9

It is by far not the worst regex I have seen, but it takes time for me to interpret it. What if we could add some whitespaces around it?

Only Perl 6 allows whitespaces for formatting by default. Unfortunately, whitespaces in other dialects are literal characters that match themselves.

Not everything is lost, though. In this chapter, we will turn seemingly nonsense regular expressions that are impossible to read into maintainable code. We will investigate the possible solutions for creating maintainable regular expressions.

# Extended Mode

PCRE and some ERE languages allow an extended mode. The syntax is as follows:

```
/(?x) regex      # comment line 1
      body       # comment line 2
      in         # comment line 3
      extended   # comment line 4
      mode       # comment line 5
/
```

In extended mode, whitespaces do not match anything; they are just there for formatting. The hash character (#) indicates the start of a comment, lasting until the end of the line.

(?x) should be the first thing in the regular expression. You cannot just turn extended mode on in the middle of the expression. The construct (?x) is actually a regex flag or modifier. In some dialects or regex libraries, instead of writing /a/i, you can use the construct /(i)a/. The advantage of placing regex modifiers at the front is readability. When an expression is long, readers prefer knowing the modifiers before reading the expression itself.

I highly recommend turning on extended mode. Recall the following expression:

```
/^(?=.*[A-Z].*[A-Z])(?=.*[!@#$&*])(?=.*[0-9].*[0-9])
(?=.*[a-z].*[a-z]).{8,}$/
```

The following is the extended mode equivalent of the same expression:

```
/(?x)
   ^                    # Start anchor
   (?=.*[A-Z].*[A-Z])   # At least two upper case letters
   (?=.*[!@#$&*])        # AND at least one special character
   (?=.*[0-9].*[0-9])    # AND at least two digits
   (?=.*[a-z].*[a-z])    # AND at least two lower case letters
   .{8,}                 # String is at least 8 characters long
   $                     # End anchor
/
```

Believe it or not, this is the same expression as the previous one-liner.

Unfortunately, not all dialects have extended mode. For instance, in EMACS and VIM, you don't have it. In JavaScript, extended mode is not available either, but you can use the XRegExp library[3] to turn on extended mode.

```
const regex = new XRegExp( '                                   \
   ^                    # Start anchor                          \
   (?=.*[A-Z].*[A-Z])   # At least two upper case letters       \
   (?=.*[!@#$&*])        # AND at least one special character    \
   (?=.*\\d.*\\d)        # AND at least two digits               \
   (?=.*[a-z].*[a-z])    # AND at least two lower case letters   \
   .{8,}                 # String is at least 8 characters long  \
   $                     # End anchor                            \
');
```

---

[3]https://github.com/slevithan/xregexp

Don't forget to escape backslashes when you use the XRegExp constructor. To illustrate this, I used \\d instead of [0-9].

Even without extended mode, if you think outside the box, you can make your code more maintainable. For instance, using the RegExp constructor of JavaScript and using the syntax of the JavaScript language, you can write code that is easy to read.

```
const regex = new RegExp(
    '^'                    + // Start anchor
    '(?=.*[A-Z].*[A-Z])' + // At least two upper case letters
    '(?=.*[!@#$&*])'      + // AND at least one special character
    '(?=.*\\d.*\\d)'      + // AND at least two digits
    '(?=.*[a-z].*[a-z])' + // AND at least two lower case letters
    '.{8,}'                + // String is at least 8 characters
                                 long
    '$'                      // End anchor
);
```

# Regex Subroutines

A few regex dialects provide subroutines. Subroutines are like functions in programming languages. Your regex becomes more readable if you don't specify the whole expression as one chunk and instead you abstract some pieces of the expression into subroutines. Your expression also becomes more DRY (Don't Repeat Yourself). After all, copying and pasting the same subroutine three or four times in an expression is not too maintainable.

A subroutine is executed whenever it is called from any point of the expression. If the subroutine is matched, execution of the regular expression is followed as usual. If the subroutine is not matched, backtracking takes place.

# PCRE Subroutines

Check out the documentation of your regex host language in the case
of PCRE. Not all PCRE languages support subroutines. In the case of
JavaScript, for instance, I suggest using the XRegExp library to enhance the
expressive power of your regular expressions.

```
var time = XRegExp.build('(?x)^ {{hours}} ({{minutes}}) $', {
  hours: XRegExp.build('{{h12}} : | {{h24}}', {
    h12: /1[0-2]|0?[1-9]/,
    h24: /2[0-3]|[01][0-9]/
  }, 'x'),
  minutes: /^[0-5][0-9]$/
});
```

The {{hours}}, {{minutes}}, {{h12}}, and {{h24}} placeholders
insert subexpressions in their own place.

XRegExp subroutines look a bit complex. The generic PCRE subroutine
syntax is a bit easier to read.

```
(?(DEFINE)
    (?<SUBROUTINE1>
        # body of SUBROUTINE1
    )
    (?<SUBROUTINE2>
        # body of SUBROUTINE2
    )
)
```

The DEFINE section of an expression never matches anything. It is used
to declare your subroutines.

Use (?&SUBROUTINE1) inside your expression to match it.

Let's see an example matching a currency symbol and a price that may contain a whole part and a fractional part. We assume that there is room for up to two digits in the fractional part.

```
/(?x) (?&CURRENCY) (?&PRICE)

    (?(DEFINE)
      (?<CURRENCY> [\$\€] )
      (?<PRICE>     \d++ \.?+ \d{0,2} )
    )
/
```

# Perl 6 Subroutines

The Perl 6 syntax for subroutines is cleaner than the PCRE syntax, but it works more or less in the same way as the PCRE version.

You can declare Perl 6 subroutines in the following way:

```
/
    :my regex SUBROUTINE1 {
        # body of SUBROUTINE1
    }

    :my regex SUBROUTINE2 {
        # body of SUBROUTINE2
    }
/
```

You can call a subroutine inside your Perl 6 expression with `<SUBROUTINE1>`.

Let's rewrite the same currency example you saw in the "PCRE Subroutines" section.

```
/(?x) (?&CURRENCY) (?&PRICE)

    (?(DEFINE)
      (?<CURRENCY>  [\$\€] )
      (?<PRICE>     \d++ \.?+ \d**0..2 )
    )
/
```

# Recursion and Circular References with Subroutines

As you can call subroutines from subroutines, you can use them to create a recursive structure.

You can even formulate circular references with subroutines, so you can call subroutine B from A, and you can call subroutine A from B.

Be aware, though, that you may increase the level of nondeterminism with these constructs, making your expression less efficient.

# Extended Mode, Subroutines, and Abstractions

*Abstraction* is the act of identifying reusable code and extracting this code out to one place. We can create subroutines to abstract repeated pieces of functionality in our regular expressions, and we can reuse them as many times as we want. Subroutines are essential in writing maintainable DRY regular expressions.

With the benefits of extended mode, you will be able to say goodbye to long, unmaintainable regex riddles. You could even consider writing regular expressions that are thousands of characters long with full clarity. Just imagine, before you picked up this book, you might have had trouble reading a 20-character expression.

# Named Capture Groups

In PCRE, we extract the values of capture groups with \1, \2, and so on. The number of the capture group is based on the order of the opening parenthesis belonging to the capture group from left to right.

We are now doing our best to make our regular expressions maintainable. Just imagine what happens if someone decides to add a pair of parentheses in our regular expression. Has this ever happened to you? If yes, you know how inconvenient it is. One change may affect the reference of all your capture groups in the expression. This goes against the principles of maintainability because there is *tight coupling* between the position of the parentheses inside the expression and the code surrounding the regular expression, geared at processing the value of the capture groups.

Our primary goal in this section is to fix the name of the capture groups. Our secondary goal is to make these names semantic.

If named captures exist in your dialect, use them for better maintainability.

## EMACS Named Capture Groups

EMACS makes it possible to fix the number of the capture group: \(?1: .* \). This name is not semantic, as we still have to stick to numbers.

## PCRE Named Capture Groups

In PCRE, we can use proper names for capture groups: (?<VARIABLE_NAME> .* ). In the languages allowing named capture groups, it is possible to use these names in the code surrounding the regular expression to extract these capture groups.

For instance, in Python, we have learned that match.group( 1 ) gives us the value of the first capture group. Instead of the number, we can also pass the name of a named capture group. match.group( 'VARIABLE_NAME' ) extracts the capture group with the name VARIABLE_NAME.

In JavaScript, ES2018 comes with named capture groups. Let's solve the example we saw in the Capture Groups section, where we matched the price and the currency symbol of a label. This time, our solution will be maintainable because we will use named capture groups.

**Exercise 1**: Suppose we would like to retrieve the currency, the numeric price value, and the full price with a currency symbol in a string of the following format:

```
Price: €19.00
```

The regular expression matching this string is as follows:

```
/^Price: [€\$]\d\d\.\d\d$/
```

We have to escape the dollar sign as a currency symbol, because $ is a meta character denoting an end-of-string or end-of-line anchor. We also have to escape the dot because it is a meta character denoting one arbitrary character.

After adding some parentheses to capture the values we want, the regular expression looks like this:

```
/^Price: (([€\$])(\d\d\.\d\d))$/
```

We have three capture groups to access the data, as shown in Table 9-1.

*Table 9-1.* *Capture Groups*

| Capture Group Number | Data |
| --- | --- |
| 1 | Full price |
| 2 | Currency symbol |
| 3 | Numeric price |

From a maintainability point of view, using the indices 1, 2, and 3 to refer to these capture groups is not a brilliant idea.

Imagine, for instance, that requirements change such that `Price` may be multilingual, and you have to capture the price text in the language it appears in.

```
/^(Price|Preis): (([€\$])(\d\d\.\d\d))$/
```

Bingo. Capture groups 1, 2, and 3 became 2, 3, and 4, respectively. You have to rewrite all your code processing these values.

This is why getting fed up with numbered capture groups is a healthy feeling. Let's use capture groups to increase the maintainability of the code. Our capture groups will look like Table 9-2.

***Table 9-2.*** *Capture Groups*

| Capture Group Number | Data |
| --- | --- |
| `<fullPrice>` | Full price |
| `<currency>` | Currency symbol |
| `<numPrice>` | Numeric price |

We will use the syntax (`?<name>content`) to match `content` in the capture group name.

```
/^Price: (?<fullPrice>(?<currency>[€\$])(?<numPrice>\d\d\.\d\d))$/
```

To create a named capture group, all we need to do is write a question mark after the start of the parentheses and then put the capture group name inside greater-than and less-than symbols.

And we are done. Let's execute the solution.

```
console.table(
    /^Price: (?<fullPrice>(?<currency>[€\$])
    (?<numPrice>\d\d\.\d\d))$/
        .exec('Price: $15.99')
        .groups
)

> (index)    Value
  currency   "$"
  numPrice   "15.99"
  fullPrice  "$15.99"
```

Although you can still refer to the captured groups with their numeric indices 1, 2, and 3, you can also use their label names if you access the groups property.

Last, but not least, it is possible to formulate a backreference on the capture group name using the format \k<groupName>.

Named capture groups make your expressions more maintainable. That's their purpose.

## Perl 6 Named Capture Groups

The syntax is $<VARIABLE_NAME>=( .* ). You can retrieve its value using $<VARIABLE_NAME> in your code.

# Case Study: XRegExp Library for JavaScript

XRegExp is a powerful library that makes JavaScript regular expressions more expressive and more maintainable. If you need regular expressions on a regular basis, no pun intended, then I highly recommend including XRegExp in your application.

You can read the documentation of the library on xregexp.com, and you can clone it from GitHub.[4] You can also install XRegExp from npm, using the command npm i xregexp.

Let's do the latter and install XRegExp using npm locally in an empty folder.

Now that the installation is done, we can open our text editor, in my case atom.io; create an empty .js file in the root, and require the XRegExp library.

```
let XRegExp = require('xregexp');
```

Let's test-drive the library by creating a simple expression.

```
let regex = XRegExp('(?i)^[ab]*$');
XRegExp.exec( 'aAbB', regex );
```

In this example, you can see an XRegExp feature, leading modifiers. This feature makes modifiers easier to read because you don't have to scroll down to the end of a regular expression to identify the modifier flags.

When executing the program, you can see that the uppercase letters as well as the lowercase letters were matched.

Let's continue talking about maintainability. A necessary condition for creating maintainable regexes is the ability to add some spacing around the expression. We can turn off the evaluation of whitespace characters with the x flag. This means we can format tokens of our expressions in any way we like, without changing its meaning. As you can see, the start anchor, the main loop, and the end anchor are now in different lines, and after execution, the pattern is still matched against the string correctly.

```
let XRegExp = require('xregexp');

let regex = XRegExp(`(?ix)
    ^
```

---

[4]https://github.com/slevithan/xregexp

```
    [ab]*
    $
`);
let result = XRegExp.exec( 'aAbB', regex );

console.log( result );
```

We have whitespaces turned off, but we can do more. We can insert some comments to make the expression more semantic. Just think about it. Some expressions are long, so why not explain them token by token?

```
let XRegExp = require('xregexp');

let regex = XRegExp(`(?ix)
  ^       # start anchor
  [ab]*   # any number of a, b, A, B characters
  $       # end anchor
`);
let result = XRegExp.exec( 'aAbB', regex );

console.log( result );
```

After the comments have been added, the solution is still working.

Now that we are aware of the extended format, let's increase the maintainability of the expression even further by adding some subpatterns.

To add a subpattern, we have to use the build method of XRegExp and specify an object with the subpattern names as keys, and the values to be inserted as values.

```
let XRegExp = require('xregexp');

let regex = XRegExp.build(`(?ix)
  ^              # start anchor
  {{charLoop}}   # any number of a, b, A, B characters
  $              # end anchor
```

```
`, {
    charLoop: /[ab]*/
} );
```

```
console.log( XRegExp.exec( 'abAB', regex ) );
```

You can see the regex was built correctly.

In fact, if you use the source property of the regex, you can see the assembled regular expression.

```
console.log( regex.source() )
```

These subpatterns work like subroutines, and they are useful in general when it comes to creating larger regular expressions.

This was a short introduction to the XRegExp library. You have seen the maintainability enhancements of regexes, and there are some more features that are available to you. Interestingly, many of the ES2018 updates were based on features already available in XRegExp, so XRegExp was an innovator in this sense. The Unicode escapes, the dotall flag, and the named capture groups were all available in the XRegExp library, which was one reason why we used them in this chapter.

# Summary

This chapter was the icing on the cake. You can be proud of yourself because now you not only understand regular expressions but can also write maintainable expressions. These skills catapult you to the top 1 percent of software developers in terms of regular expression usage.

You have learned the following techniques to increase the maintainability of your code:

- Using extended mode to introduce whitespaces and comments

- Using subroutines to create named abstractions in your code

- Using named capture groups to make the retrieval of your capture groups maintainable

In the next chapter, you will learn how to optimize your regular expressions.

# CHAPTER 10

# Optimizing Regular Expressions

You have learned all the tools to optimize the execution of a regular expression; therefore, this chapter acts as a summary for everything you have learned so far.

You learned that the execution of regexes can be modeled using two types of automata: deterministic and nondeterministic FSM.

The execution time of a nondeterministic automaton can be exponentially measured in the number of its steps. The complexity comes from the need for backtracking.

Creating a deterministic finite state automaton from a nondeterministic automaton also has exponential complexity.

In most execution environments, regular expression virtual machines follow the nondeterministic model. This is because success may be a lot faster than failure. We could just match the input in $n$ steps, where $n$ is the size of the input. If we made our execution deterministic, the state space could explode, and we could end up with $O(\ 2\ \text{^}\ n\ )$ complexity.

Using a nondeterministic model has consequences. We will make use of these consequences while optimizing our regexes.

© Zsolt Nagy 2018
Z. Nagy, *Regex Quick Syntax Reference*, https://doi.org/10.1007/978-1-4842-3876-9_10

# Summary of the Optimization Techniques

As complexity arises from backtracking, the intended goal of optimization techniques is to *minimize backtracking*. We will consider a few ways to do that.

- Making character classes more specific

- Repeating character class loops

- Using possessive repeat modifiers

- Using atomic groups

- Refactoring for optimization

Some compilers perform automatic optimizations on your regexes. The generic rule is that you are left on your own.

# Making Character Classes More Specific

Our enemy is the `.*` pattern because in the worst case you may end up backtracking as many times as the length of your input.

For instance, suppose you want to capture identifier names in between the microtemplate tags ${ and }. In this example, we assume we are looking for patterns of form ${ id }, where id may not contain whitespaces. The following extended PCRE expression does the trick:

```
/(?x)
    \$\{  # Consume the opening tag ${
    \s*   # Consume all whitespaces greedily
    (.+?) # Minimal match our identifier
    \s*   # Consume all remaining whitespaces greedily
    \}    # Close the tag
/
```

Notice the extended mode (?x). Remember, starting a regex with (?x) makes whitespace characters not match themselves and allows you to place comments in the expression followed by a # character until a newline character.

As we are looking for identifier characters, we are sure that these characters are not whitespaces, and they are not closing braces either. Therefore, it is a luxury to use the arbitrary character class here. We can make our expression more deterministic by changing .+? to a more specific character class: [^\s\}].

```
/(?x)
    \$\{          # Consume the opening tag ${
    \s*           # Consume all whitespaces greedily
    ([^\s\}]+)    # Minimal match our identifier
    \s*           # Consume all remaining whitespaces greedily
    \}            # Close the tag
/
```

Notice that we now have the luxury to use a greedy repeat modifier because it does not matter whether we are greedy or lazy. In fact, our best bet is just to go for a possessive repeat modifier, but let's not jump ahead of ourselves too much.

---

**Tip**   When using alternative execution or a character class, none of the choices in the alternation may start with the same character as the character followed by the alternation.

---

Avoid [xy]*x. Understand the requirements better because there is almost always an easier solution: /[xy]*x/ matches a substring of the input that contains x and y characters only and ends with x. If we just check for the existence of such a pattern, checking for /y*x/ is sufficient.

If our task is to verify /^[xy]*x$/, go for /^(y*+x)*+$/. We possessively match any number of y characters, followed by an x. We look for as many of these patterns as possible. As we used possessive matching everywhere, there is absolutely no backtracking present in this expression. To allow the usage of possessive loops, we had to eliminate the [xy] character set by factoring x out of it.

# Repeating Character Class Loops

Avoid repeating the same character class loop, regardless of whether you use the greedy or lazy version.

```
/(?x)
    \$\{    # Consume the opening tag ${
    \s*     # Consume all whitespaces greedily
    (.+?)   # Minimal match our identifier
    \s*     # Consume all remaining whitespaces greedily
    \}      # Close the tag
/
```

Here, (\s*)(.+?)(\s*) is an invitation for trouble. If, for any reason, we don't find the } character in our input string, the regular expression goes into backtracking hell and tries every possible combination of including each possible sequence of whitespace characters either in one of the \s* patterns or in the .+? pattern.

You have already seen a possible solution to eliminate this backtracking hell.

```
/(?x)
    \$\{        # Consume the opening tag ${
    \s*         # Consume all whitespaces greedily
    ([^\s\}]+)  # Minimal match our identifier
    \s*         # Consume all remaining whitespaces greedily
    \}          # Close the tag
/
```

By making the character class in the middle distinct from the other two, we will not allow the regex VM to go on a Don Quixote windmill fight of trying to determine where our whitespaces belong.

To eliminate all backtracking whatsoever, we can use another technique, covered next.

# Use Possessive Repeat Modifiers Whenever Possible

Possessive repeat modifiers never backtrack by definition; they fail instead. In exchange for eliminating backtracking, we limit the state space by not exploring the backtracking branches at all.

```
/(?x)
    \$\{        # Consume the opening tag ${
    \s*+        # Consume all whitespaces greedily
    ([^\s\}]+)  # Minimal match our identifier
    \s*+        # Consume all remaining whitespaces greedily
    \}          # Close the tag
/
```

Here the regex engine won't even try backtracking in the case of the \s*+ pattern. This is because we as humans know that if there is no }, it does not matter how we match the whitespaces. Therefore, we can simply accelerate the failure.

Remember the rule for discovering the opportunity to add possessive repeat modifiers:

> If the character following the possessive loop is mutually exclusive with the first character of the pattern inside the loop, then you may consider using a possessive loop.

# Use Atomic Groups

Not only loops but also alternations can backtrack in an inefficient way. We might have already matched a node in an alternation, just to find that at a later stage we examine the same character, trying to match other branches of the same alternation.

I can illustrate atomic groups with an easy example from my personal life. I tend to lose stuff easily. Sometimes I go look for my stuff in my house. For instance, suppose I am looking for my phone. I look at the table, my pocket, and also the kitchen.

Once I find my phone, I check whether I have an appointment. I have appointments on Tuesday. If the day does not match, I don't need my phone anymore.

The following regular expression captures first me looking for my phone and then checking the day:

```
/(?>table|pocket|kitchen) --> Tuesday/
```

Suppose on Wednesday I find my phone in my pocket, and then I figure out it's not Thursday, so I have to backtrack. Then I go back and look for my phone in the kitchen. This doesn't make any sense! Once I have found my phone, it would make sense to *stop looking for my phone*. This is what atomic groups solve.

For instance, suppose you would like to get an exact match for list, lost, or lust. In PCRE,

```
/^(list|lost|lust)$/
```

Suppose we are trying to match the text lists. We start at the first branch of the alternation and match list completely. Given we have yet to parse an s character instead of terminating the sequence, we backtrack. Now we are back to square one, with the string lists, and we try to match it against lost. After consuming the l character, we have to backtrack. In the third branch, the same thing happens: we match the l character just to conclude that we need an i instead of a u.

This time, we got away with unnecessary backtracking cheaply. Imagine, though, what happens if backtracking operations are nested. What happens if there is a complex subexpression in the place of the l character. We can waste a lot of resources.

This is why it makes perfect sense to treat this alternation in a possessive way. Both PCRE and Perl 6 make it possible to create *atomic groups*, also known as *possessive groups*. In a possessive group, if any of the branches match, execution does not go back to try another branch. If we try to backtrack into a possessive group, we automatically fail the expression. Once you leave a possessive group, you cannot backtrack into it.

```
PCRE:    /(?> a|b)/
Perl 6:  / [ a|b ]: /
```

Notice that in Perl 6, the colon is consistent for loops and alternations. Perl 6 appears to be cleaner than PCRE in this sense. In most programming languages, we still deal with the PCRE syntax, so you will have to get used to the PCRE syntax if you want to use possessive groups.

If you have ever written Prolog programs, a possessive group is like the *cut* (!) operation. It cuts execution branches from the theorem proving tree.

> Use possessive groups whenever all alternatives in
> an *or* construct are mutually exclusive.

Let's finish with the execution of our previous example. We try to match lists against the regex.

```
/^(?> list|lost|lust)$/
```

We are in the first branch and match list. We leave the possessive alternation. There is still an s character left, and given we were supposed to be at the end of the string, we backtrack. Given we cannot backtrack into the possessive group, this regular expression fails to match lists. Problem solved.

# Refactor for Optimization

We saw this optimization technique in action when we first introduced the list, lost, lust example. We can factor out common characters at the beginning and at the end of the expression. This regex

```
/^(list|lost|lust)$/
```

becomes the following:

```
/^l(i|o|u)st$/
```

Matching also becomes more efficient because after backtracking, we don't have to match the same character over and over again.

Once you have only one character in each branch of your alternation, you can use character sets for higher efficiency.

```
/^l[iou]st$/
```

# Optimization Techniques Limit Nondeterministic Execution

Optimization techniques are all about cutting down execution paths from an execution tree. You can optimize an expression up to the extent that it becomes deterministic.

A necessary condition for creating a deterministic execution plan of a regular expression is to

- Factor out all prefixes in alternations

- Make all your loops and alternations possessive

# Summary

After learning how to write maintainable regular expressions, the next task was to write efficient regexes. I covered the following optimization techniques:

- Making character classes more specific

- Repeating character class loops

- Using possessive repeat modifiers

- Using atomic groups

- Refactoring for optimization

All of these optimization techniques are geared toward making execution of your regular expressions more deterministic.

# CHAPTER 11

# Parsing HTML Code and URL Query Strings with Regular Expressions

In this chapter, we will use JavaScript to parse an HTML document and process the query string of a URL.

## Parsing HTML Tags

**Exercise 1**: Suppose an HTML document is given. Extract all the `<td>` tags using a regular expression, and print their content to the console. You can assume any content including newline characters inside the `<td>` tags. The `<td>` tags may have attributes.

**Example Input:**

```
const table = `
    <table>
        <tr>
            <td class="first">text 1</td>
```

```
        <TD>text 2</TD>
    </tr>
    <tr>
        <td>text trés</td>
        <td>
            text 4 first line
            text 4 second line
        </td>
        <td></td>
    </tr>
 </table>`;
```

**Solution:**

When dealing with a multiline regular expression, it is worth using the new ES2018 s (dotall) flag to treat the whole text as a single line. Given there are multiple table details to match, we will definitely need to declare our regular expression as global using the g flag.

```
/.*/gs.exec( table )
```

Let's also add the opening and closing tags that we would like to match. Notice there are four distinct options matching a table detail element: <td>, <Td>, <tD>, and <TD>. We can match them all with just one expression, without any alternation or character sets, by declaring our regular expression as case insensitive using the i flag. When matching the close tag </td>, make sure you escape the slash.

```
/<td>.*<\/td>/gis.exec( table )
```

After executing this expression, you can see that three table details got returned as one. There are multiple reasons for this error.

- First, `.*` is greedy, and it matches all characters, including other `</td>` flags and `<td>` flags. We reduce the matched string only after backtracking character by character and unlooping the characters of the last `</td>` tag.

- Second, `<td class="first">` is not matched by this regular expression because a greater-than symbol has to follow the d in the `<td>` tag according to our expression.

We can solve both problems easily.

Regarding the first problem, we can make the greedy `.*` loop lazy by adding a ? after it. These mechanics will attempt a minimal match. An alternative solution is to change `.` to `[^<]`, but this solution would imply we cannot nest tags inside `<td>`, so that is not a brilliant idea.

The second problem can be addressed by matching all characters between the td and the >. In this case, we know the characters we match are distinct from >. Therefore, we match any number of non-greater-than characters in a `[^>]*` loop.

```
/<td[^>]*>.*?<\/td>/gis.exec( table )
```

We need one more change: we have to capture the contents of the tag so that we can access it and print it to the console.

```
let regex = /<td[^>]*>(.*?)<\/td>/gis

let contents = '';
while ( contents = regex.exec( table ) ) {
    console.log( contents[1] );
}
```

Note the contents of the last table detail are captured as undefined.

# Processing the Query String of a URL

**Exercise 2**: Create a regex that transforms the query string of a URL into an object of key-value pairs such that

```
?key1=value1&key2=value2&...&keyN=valueN
```

becomes the following:

```
{
    key1: 'value1',
    key2: 'value2',
    ...
    keyN: 'valueN'
}
```

You can assume the text starts with a question mark.

The lengths of the keys are all positive. The lengths of the values are non-negative. The equation sign is always present.

**Solution:**

First we have to read a question mark or an ampersand, followed by an arbitrary list of characters of positive length that are not equation signs. We have to capture the characters after the ampersand.

```
/[?&]([^=])+/g
```

Then we match an equation sign, followed by any number of characters that are not ampersands. We have to capture these characters.

```
/[?&]([^=])+=([^&]*)/g
```

Each key ends up in capture group 1, and each value ends up in capture group 2. As the expression is global, we will match the key-value pairs one by one.

144

We will now create the result object using JavaScript.

```
let queryParameters = {};
let queryString = '?key1=value1&key2=value2&key3=&key4=value4';
let regex = /[?&]([^=]+)+=([^&]*)/g;
let result = null;

while ( result = regex.exec( queryString ) ) {
    queryParameters[ result[1] ] = result[2];
}

console.log( queryParameters );
```

# This Is Not the End, but the Beginning

Wow, you have come a long way. You can consider yourself a champion of regular expressions. Let's recap the steps you went through in this book.

- *An Introduction to Regular Expressions*: You found out why most people never master regular expressions. After identifying and busting some myths about regular expressions, you started getting some hands-on practice in multiple regex dialects.

- *Regex Syntax 101*: You equipped yourself with some basic building blocks that enable you to write basic regular expressions.

- *Executing Regular Expressions*: Enough about theory! It was time to get some hands-on practice in ten PCRE-based languages. You learned how to test and execute your code in the browser, without installing any development environments.

- *Visualizing Regex Execution Using Finite State Machines*: This chapter was a game changer. Finite state machines show you how regular expressions are executed. You got an in-depth understanding about the regexes you wrote up to this point.

© Zsolt Nagy 2018
Z. Nagy, *Regex Quick Syntax Reference*, https://doi.org/10.1007/978-1-4842-3876-9

- *Repeat Modifiers*: Although I could have covered repeat modifiers earlier, I waited for this chapter until you managed to understand the finite state machine model of regexes. Finite state machines add a deeper understanding to using the different types of repeat modifiers.

- *Character Sets and Character Classes*: Character sets and classes are vital when it comes to writing compact and efficient regular expressions.

- *Substring Extraction from Regular Expressions*: This was your first advanced topic. You learned how to create capture groups and extract substrings from regular expressions.

- *Lookahead and Lookbehind*: There are times when you want to match a character sequence if it is right before or right after another sequence. This is where these constructs become useful.

- *Maintaining Regular Expressions*: This was the icing on the cake. You learned how to write maintainable regular expressions, allowing you to create regexes that are hundreds or even thousands of characters long. You also learned how to optimize your expressions for deterministic execution.

- *Optimizing Regular Expressions*: This chapter summarized different optimization techniques that limit nondeterminism in the execution of regular expressions by cutting the state space.

- *Parsing HTML Code and URL Query Strings with Regular Expressions*: This chapter showed you how to use JavaScript to parse an HTML document and process the query string of a URL.

The promise of this book was that you would get an in-depth understanding of regular expressions, allowing you to

- Understand the imperative elements of the language

- Write maintainable code

- Write efficient code

- Not get lost in the process

Now you have all the tools required to write regular expressions that are easy to create, maintain, verify, test, and debug.

# "What If I Want to Learn More?"

Send me a message about the specific context in which you would like to use regular expressions. You can reach me at info@zsoltnagy.eu.

I have recorded a JavaScript video course on regular expressions, including the library XRegExp. Once proper demand arises, I will create other regex video courses or books.

I also recommend that you check out my YouTube channel.[1] The following resources may be especially interesting to you:

- A playlist on regular expression videos[2]

- A JavaScript interview exercise, where regexes simplify the code[3]

---

[1] https://tinyurl.com/zsoltnagy
[2] https://tinyurl.com/regex-playlist
[3] https://tinyurl.com/js-interview-regex

# Keep in Touch

You can read regular articles from me on

- zsoltnagy.eu,[4] a blog on writing maintainable web applications
- devcareermastery.com,[5] a career blog on designing a fulfilling career

Sign up to my e-mail list for regular free content. I am the author of these two books:

- *ES6 in Practice : The Complete Developer's Guide*[6]

- *The Developer's Edge: How to Double Your Career Speed with Soft-Skills*[7]

Check them out if these topics are interesting to you.

---

[4]http://zsoltnagy.eu
[5]http://devcareermastery.com
[6]https://leanpub.com/es6-in-practice
[7]https://leanpub.com/thedevelopersedge

# Index

## A
Arbitrary character, 13

## B
Backtracking, 55–56

## C, D, E
Character classes, 148
Character sets, 85–86, 148
   classes, 88–91
   concatenation, 92–93
   exclusions from, 88
   [01] expression, 86
   ranges, 87–88

## F, G
Finite state machines (FSMs), 53
   /ab/, 54–55
   automatically generating
      regex, 63, 65–66
   backtracking, 55–56
   basic regex simplifications, 62
   deterministic and
      nondeterministic
      regex modeling, 56–61

   successful match, 63
   visualizing regex execution, 147

## H, I
HTML tags, parsing, 141–143, 149

## J, K
JavaScript regular expressions
   ES6 unicode regular
      expressions, 31–32
   global matching, 28–29
   multiline matches, 30
   regex modifiers, 27–28
   RegExp methods, 25
   sticky matches, 32–33
   string methods, 26–27

## L
Literal characters, 10
Lookahead string, 109, 148
   scores, 111–112
   string abc, 110
   syntax, 110
Lookbehind string, 112, 148
   syntax, 112
   using PCRE, 113

# M, N

Maintainance, regular
    expressions, 148
  extended mode, 116–118
  named capture groups, 122
    EMACS, 122
    PCRE, 122–125
    Perl 6, 125
    tight coupling, 122
  regex subroutines, 118
    extended mode, subroutines,
      and abstractions, 121
    PCRE subroutines, 119
    Perl 6 subroutines, 120
    recursion and circular
      references, 121
  XRegExp, 125–128
Meta characters, 10–12
Modifiers, 27

# O

Optimization, 148
  character classes, 132–134
  deterministic model, 131
  limit nondeterministic
    execution, 138
  to minimize backtracking, 132
  nondeterministic model, 131
  possessive repeat modifiers, 135
  refactor for, 138
  repeating character
    class loops, 134–135
  use atomic groups, 136–137

# P

Perl Compatible Regular
    Expressions (PCRE), 7
execution environments,
    programming languages
  C#, 44–45
  C++, 49–51
  Golang, 48–49
  Java, 41–43
  Perl 5, 40–41
  PHP, 35–37
  Python, 37–40
  R, 43–44
  Ruby, 46–47

# Q

Query string of URL, 144–145
Query strings, 149

# R

Regex syntax 101, 147
  formulating expression
    alternative execution, 14
    anchored start and
      end, 15–18
    arbitrary character class, 13
    concatenation, 14
    literal and meta
      characters, 10–12
    modifiers, 19–21
    operator precedence and
      parentheses, 15

Regular expressions
    frustrations with, 4–5
    imperative, 5–6
    importance, 1–2
    JavaScript, 3
    language family, 6–8
    search patterns, 2
Repeat modifiers, 68, 148
    backtracking, 68–70
    branching, 67
    fixed-range
        matching, 74–77
    greedy, 78–79
    lazy, 79–82
    loop exactly n times, 77
    loops, 67
    matching any number
        of times, 73–74
    matching at least one a
        character, 70–72

matching at most once, 72–73
possessive, 82–83

## S, T, U, V, W, X, Y, Z

Simple regular expressions (SRE), 6
Substring extraction, 148
    capture groups, 96–97
        extensions, 108
        and performance, 106–108
        Perl 6, 97–98
    retrieval of captured
        substrings, 98
        data, 99
        JavaScript, 100
        Perl 5, 103–104
        PHP, 101
        Python, 102
    reusing captured substrings
        within regex, 104–106

Printed in the United States
By Bookmasters